The Pocket Encyclopedia of
CHRYSANTHEMUMS
in Color

The Pocket Encyclopedia of

CHRYSANTHEMUMS

in Color

by
STANLEY GOSLING

ARCO PUBLISHING COMPANY, INC.
NEW YORK

Published 1973 by Arco Publishing Company, Inc.
219 Park Avenue South, New York, N.Y. 10003
Copyright © 1971 by Blandford Press Ltd.
All rights reserved
Library of Congress Catalog Card Number 72-94233
ISBN 0-668-02913-7
Printed in Great Britain

LIST OF CONTENTS

FOREWORD

I know of no flower which will respond so well to good culture as the chrysanthemum; hence the fascination it holds for countless enthusiasts who grow for exhibition, and its popularity as a flower for garden or house decoration.

Many books have been written about the chrysanthemum in recent years by both professional and amateur growers, but few writers have the experience and knowledge of Stanley Gosling who, in his position as Secretary of the National Chrysanthemum Society, lives in a world of chrysanthemums: growing, lecturing, judging and answering countless letters requesting advice on the subject.

To be a good writer on general horticultural matters one needs to have some of the attributes of the antique dealer who knows a little about a lot, but to be a specialist in any field one needs to know a lot about a little. Stanley Gosling certainly knows a great deal about chrysanthemums, and in this extremely interesting book all aspects of growing for exhibition or private pleasure are dealt with in his usual capable manner. This is a book for both the garden and the greenhouse enthusiast, for the reader who would like to grow blooms a little better than his neighbour, or for the grower who wishes to excel on the show bench. Think of any question about the cultivation of chrysanthemums and you will find the answer in this book. Stanley Gosling's lists and descriptions of the leading cultivars are most informative and helpful and the illustrations are probably the finest, most numerous and correct to colour of any publication to date.

I can recommend this book to all chrysanthemum lovers; I know its possession will give much pleasure and stimulate great interest, and that it will hold pride of place as an accurate and comprehensive guide to all chrysanthemum problems.

Harry James
Chairman, National Chrysanthemum Society

ACKNOWLEDGEMENTS

The Author and Publishers wish to make acknowledgement to the following:

Mr. E. L. Crowson, A.I.I.P., F.R.P.S. who photographed the great majority of the illustrations.

Mr. Frank Rowe, for permission to photograph chrysanthemums at Rylands Nurseries, Wellington, Somerset.

The Royal Horticultural Society, for the most generous co-operation of the staff at the R.H.S. Trial Grounds, Wisley, Surrey, where extensive use was made of the Trial Grounds for the photographing of many of the chrysanthemums.

Mr. John R. Bell, of Horam, Sussex, for supplying photographs.

Messrs. Elmhouse Nurseries, Wisbech, Cambridgeshire for the loan of photographs.

Mr. J. F. Smith, of Sidcup, Kent for the loan of photographs.

Mr. H. Randall, of Bushey, Herts for the loan of photographs.

Mr. A. J. Wren, of Broxbourne, Herts for the loan of photographs.

The National Chrysanthemum Society, for permission to reproduce colour photographs from the Society's collection.

THE NATIONAL CHRYSANTHEMUM SOCIETY

Since its establishment in 1846 the National Chrysanthemum Society has devoted much time, thought and energy to the improvement and popularisation of the Chrysanthemum. The Society caters for all chrysanthemum growers – for those who cultivate for personal pleasure, or for exhibition purposes.

Fellows of the Society receive a Year Book, four Quarterly Bulletins, and Passes to Shows.

Particulars of fellowship can be obtained from the Secretary, 65 St. Margaret's Avenue, Whetstone, London N.20.

INTRODUCTION

The perennial autumn-flowering chrysanthemums, now so popular with amateur gardeners, commercial growers and florists, are complex hybrids derived from several species of chrysanthemum that grow wild in China and Japan. Over 2,000 years have passed since man first began to cultivate the chrysanthemum and the precise ancestors of the modern cultivated chrysanthemum (*C.morifolium*) cannot now be determined.

The original Chinese cultivars were practically all cultivars with tightly incurved types of flower and there was a very limited range of colour: mainly white, yellow and pale mauve. On the other hand, the reflexed, tightly and loosely incurving types of chrysanthemum which have been developed by chrysanthemum breeders in England, France, Australia and the United States from cultivars originally introduced from Japan, have a very wide range of colour and are today numbered in thousands.

During the past thirty years, chrysanthemum breeders have by hybridisation introduced new strains giving much improved standards of quality together with a wide range of colour shades and forms. Chrysanthemums have a flowering period extending over five months when grown under natural conditions. Few other flowers can compare with their lasting qualities as blooms remain in good condition on individual plants for at least a month and, when cut and used for floral arrangements, they will keep fresh for two to three weeks. It can be justly claimed that the chysanthemum is the Queen of Autumn flowers.

In this book the cultivars illustrated in colour number approximately 350 and are selected from those of proven popularity and reliability. They cover a comprehensive range selected from each section of the chrysanthemum classification. In addition to the colour illustrations, which are named, there are also comprehensive descriptions which give the height, habit, flowering period and suitability of each plant illustrated. They are divided into Part 1, Early-flowering Chrysanthemums, followed by Part 2, October-flowering, Mid-season and Late-flowering Chrysanthemums.

So far as cultivation is concerned, there is nothing simpler. Chrysanthemums virtually grow themselves, but the degree of excellence

9

obtained is in direct proportion to the state of growing conditions and care and attention given at the appropriate times. These will of course vary according to the country in which they are grown, and the dates mentioned for growing in England will need to be adapted for other countries.

To grow chrysanthemums successfully, it is essential to have a basic knowledge of the plant's cultural requirements. Few plants will respond more to care and attention, hence the popularity of the flower with many thousands of amateur growers where the environmental conditions are naturally suitable or can be made suitable.

The chapters dealing with cultivation cover the complete life cycle of the plant from the unrooted cutting stage to the mature blooms at their respective maximum potential. Within this rather wide arc are: selection of stock plants and winter care; propagation; soils; potting composts and fertilisers; preparation of the growing ground; watering and feeding, and stopping and timing.

Half-tone illustrations and line drawings are used to illustrate the various aspects of cultivation.

This book is primarily for those who are new to chrysanthemum growing, the colour illustrations will help them to select the cultivars they wish to grow. Yet many established growers should find it very useful, for it may introduce them to cultivars they have not previously grown and, within the chapters on cultivation, to methods that may enable them to obtain even better results than hitherto.

1. CHRYSANTHEMUM TECHNICAL TERMS

A chrysanthemum bloom is made up of a large number of small flowers or florets. These florets are of two kinds. The coloured portion of the bloom is made up of ray florets (often incorrectly called petals), and the cushion in the centre of the bloom is composed of disk florets. Pollen is produced only by the disk florets. The original wild chrysanthemums from which the present cultivated forms have been developed all had single, daisy-like flowers; but by selection and breeding the present-day double blooms (which have numerous ray florets and very few disk florets) have been developed. The flower buds which form at different stages in the growth of a chrysanthemum plant do not contain the same number of ray florets. If we are to grow chrysanthemums successfully and obtain from a plant the best blooms that it is capable of producing, it is essential that we should know which buds should be allowed to grow and develop into blooms, and which buds should be removed. In order to be able to pass on this information to others it is necessary to give particular names to the buds which form at certain stages in the growth of a chrysanthemum plant, and to give names also to the methods of controlling both the growth of the plant and the development of buds.

DEFINITIONS

It is essential that the amateur grower should understand the following technical terms that are used to describe the cultivation of chrysanthemums.

A *stool* is the root of an old plant, with a portion of the old stem and its surrounding young shoots.

A *sucker* is a rooted shoot springing from the old root.

A *cutting* is an unrooted leafy growth taken either from the old root or from the old stem.

Stopping or pinching is the act of removing the tip of a growth—either the tip of the main stem or the tip of a side growth.

To break is to branch or to send out side growth.

A *break* or a *lateral growth* is a side growth.

11

A *leaf axil* is the space between the stalk of a leaf and the stem to which it is attached.

Securing a bud is the act of removing all leaf axil shoots and unwanted buds and leaving only the bud which is to develop into a flower.

The *break bud* is the flower bud, which, if the plant is left to grow naturally, eventually appears at the end of the solitary main stem, before it branches or 'breaks'. In normal circumstances this bud shrivels and does not develop a flower.

A *natural break* is the sending out of side growths from the main stem of the plant after the break bud has appeared at the end of the main stem, and without removal of the break bud.

The *First Crown bud* is the first bud which appears at the end of a lateral growth from the main stem of the plant.

The First Crown bud is termed a *natural First Crown* when the plant has made a natural break—as distinct from a First Crown bud which appears on a plant that has been stopped, i.e. a plant that has had the tip of the main stem removed before the break bud has formed.

The First Crown bud contains the greatest number of ray florets and will give the largest bloom, though not necessarily the best bloom. In some cultivars the florets are packed so tightly in the First Crown bud that they do not open well, but develop into a rough uneven bloom. Practically all early-flowering outdoor cultivars, however, produce the best flowers from First Crown buds.

Second Crown bud. If the tips of the lateral growths from the main stem are removed (in technical terms, if the first breaks are stopped), further side growths develop in the leaf axils of these laterals. These further side growths (second breaks) then grow on (perhaps for two feet), until a bud is produced at the end of each of them. That bud is termed the Second Crown bud.

The Second Crown bud does not contain as many ray florets as the First Crown bud, but they are usually of a more intense colour and are harder in texture than the florets of First Crown buds. Second Crown buds usually develop evenly and produce symmetrical flowers of good shape, though possibly slightly smaller than First Crown flowers.

A *terminal bud* is one which develops surrounded by other flower buds—marking the end of further vegetative growth of the plant. In the case of some cultivars, the Second Crown bud is also the terminal bud.

Running on is the process of rubbing out the First Crown bud after it has formed and allowing one shoot from a leaf axil below the First Crown bud to grow on to develop a flower on the Second Crown bud. This method is

Fig. 1. Young plant. If left to grow naturally it would produce a bud at the end of the main stem. This bud is called the 'Break bud'

Fig. 2. This plant has been stopped by the removal of the tip of the main stem. Young shoots called 'breaks' or 'lateral growths' are appearing in the 'leaf axils' on the main stem

Fig. 3. The first breaks or lateral growths developing from the leaf axils on the main stem

Fig. 4. Plant almost ready for disbudding. The centre bud developing at the end of each of the six breaks is a 'First Crown bud'

useful in cases where it was intended to flower a plant on the First Crown bud and it is found that the First Crown bud has formed either on too short a stem, or too early for a Show. It is also useful when the First Crown bud has been damaged by insect pests. Running on is practised in the case of some late-flowering cultivars which give their best flowers on the Second Crown buds, but which appear to resent the stopping of the first breaks in the true sense of the words.

Counting down is the process of cutting out all breaks in excess of those required—e.g. when the exhibitor reduces the number of breaks to three or four, or when the grower for garden display 'counts down' to eight or nine breaks.

Spray is the last flowering growth consisting of one stem (not a branch) with or without a central flower or bud.

Sport is a change which sometimes occurs in an established cultivar of chrysanthemum. The change may relate to the colour, form or shape of the bloom, the vigour or habit of growth of the plant, or the normal date of flowering.

Mutation is another name for a Sport.

Seedling is a new cultivar of chrysanthemum raised from seed.

Potting compost is a mixture of loam, peat or leaf-mould, and sand, to which certain plant foods have been added in order to produce a suitable medium for use in pots in which chrysanthemums are to be grown; or alternatively a medium in which chrysanthemum cuttings can be rooted.

Lifting is the process of digging up (usually in early October) Late-flowering Chrysanthemums that have been grown in the open ground throughout the summer and transferring them to the soil in a greenhouse for flowering.

Damping is the decay and rotting of chrysanthemum blooms before maturity, arising from close humid conditions, 'still' air, and lack of ventilation.

Cultivar is the internationally agreed term used to denote a plant variant raised in a garden as a seedling or sport, or introduced from the wild and maintained in cultivation because of its garden value. In a botanical context, varieties are those plants recognised by botanists as distinct sub-divisions of species occurring in the wild. The international Latin term used for them is *varietas* (abbreviated *var.*) and it will be seen that confusion may ensue if, in the English language, the word 'variety' is used for both categories.

2. COMPOSTS

COMPOSTS FOR ROOTING OF CUTTINGS

The standard potting compost evolved by the John Innes Horticultural Institution after many hundreds of experiments, can be prepared as detailed below. This is one of the best possible composts to use for rooting of chrysanthemum cuttings. The proportions given should be strictly adhered to. The fertilizers should be accurately weighed and neither more nor less than the stated quantity should be used. Do not guess and do not attempt to improve upon the mixture.

Use a standard sized tray, 14 in. long, 8½ in. wide and 3 in. deep, as a measure. Take:

> 7 seed trays of friable loam.
> 3 seed trays of moist horticultural peat.
> 2 seed trays of dry coarse sand.
> (This totals exactly two bushels)

To the above quantity must be added:

> 3 oz hoof and horn
> 3 oz superphosphate of lime ⎫ J. I. base fertilizer
> 1½ oz sulphate of potash ⎭
> 1½ oz ground chalk or ground limestone

Sift the loam through a sieve. If the peat is purchased in a compressed bale it will be very dry and lumpy; break it down until it is free from lumps and water sparingly with a fine rose can so that it is just moist. Mix the fertilizers with the dry sand and then add the sand to the loam and peat. Mix thoroughly by turning over and over until the whole is evenly distributed. This standard compost is called **J.I.P. 1.** The items bracketed above are the ingredients of John Innes base fertilizer which can now be bought ready mixed from sundriesmen. This does not contain the ground chalk (which must not be mixed with the fertilizers until the compost is being made).

Seven and a half oz of J.I. base fertilizer can be added to 2 bushels of mixed loam, peat and sand instead of the 3 oz of hoof and horn, 3 oz of superphosphate of lime and 1½ ounces of sulphate of potash detailed above. The $1\frac{1}{2}$ oz of ground chalk or ground limestone should, of course, also be added.

POTTING COMPOSTS

J.I.P. 2

The standard John Innes compost No. 2 detailed below is suitable for making a 3-in. deep bed in a frame into which to transplant early-flowering cultivars that have been rooted in seed trays; or for potting rooted chrysanthemum cuttings of any kind in 3-in. pots.

To prepare J.I.P. 2, take the same quantities of loam, peat and sand as detailed for J.I.P. No.1, but add to the 2 bushels double the quantity of fertilizer, that is:

> 6 oz hoof and horn.
> 6 oz superphosphate of lime.
> 3 oz sulphate of potash.
> 3 oz ground chalk or ground limestone.

J.I.P. 3

To prepare compost for re-potting chrysanthemums into $4\frac{1}{2}$ or 5-in. pots, take the same quantities of loam, peat and sand, but add to the 2 bushels three times the quantity of fertilizer, that is:

> 9 oz hoof and horn.
> 9 oz superphosphate of lime.
> $4\frac{1}{2}$ oz sulphate of potash.
> $4\frac{1}{2}$ oz ground chalk or ground limestone.

J.I.P. 4

This is recommended for the final potting of chrysanthemums. Take the same quantities of loam, peat and sand as detailed for J.I.P. 1, but add to the 2 bushels four times the quantity of fertilizer, that is:

> 12 oz hoof and horn.
> 12 oz superphosphate of lime.
> 6 oz sulphate of potash.
> 6 oz ground chalk or ground limestone.

The loam for making J.I. potting composts should strictly be sterilized loam but if good unsterilized loam is used in making the above composts, it will give better results than many much more complex composts made up of ingredients which are extremely variable in quality and which have no standard measurable content of plant food.

The following modification to the John Innes formula, which increases the quantity of friable loam has been proved to be more satisfactory for growing on chrysanthemums after the rooting stage and particularly for final potting purposes:

> 8 seed trays of friable loam
> $2\frac{1}{2}$ seed trays of moist horticultural peat,
> $1\frac{1}{2}$ seed trays of dry coarse sand
> (This totals exactly 2 bushels)

U.C. SOILLESS COMPOSTS

These mixtures of sand and peat have been developed by the University of California after many years of experimentation. The Americans, like ourselves, have for a long time been using the John Innes compost, but in America as in this country good top soil is becoming more difficult to obtain.

U.C. mixtures are available in small quantities for the amateur grower. They are also comparatively easy to make up. Firstly, a very fine grade of washed sand must be used, preferably one that is not too alkaline, and a good quality granulated peat. For making up small quantities the formula is as follows:

> $2\frac{1}{2}$ bushels of peat
> $2\frac{1}{2}$ bushels of washed sand

to which should be added the following:

> 1 oz potassium nitrate,
> 1 oz potassium sulphate.
> 10 oz superphosphate,
> 10 oz of carbonate lime.

The peat should be thoroughly broken down, moistened, and well mixed with the sand, and the chemical ingredients thoroughly mixed with the peat and sand.

If plants are to be grown on in the compost for a long time, 2 lbs of dolomite lime should be added, but this is not necessary if the mixture is to be used only for rooting cuttings or raising seedlings. The mixture contains a moderate amount of available nitrogen but will require supplementary feeding within two weeks of rooting.

OTHER SOILLESS COMPOSTS

During the past few years the use of soilless composts of one kind or another has become fairly widespread, mainly because many growers have found it increasingly difficult to obtain good quality turf loam at a reasonable price. Soilless composts are marketed under the brand names of various specialist manufacturers.

The bulk material in most soilless composts is peat with other plant foods added, according to the formula evolved by the manufacturers. As with most new introductions these soilless composts are being continually improved. Chrysanthemum cuttings will root quite satisfactorily in this material, and many growers have obtained good results when growing on plants to the flowering stage in large pots.

For Early-flowering chrysanthemums, grown and flowered in the open, it is not recommended to use soilless composts after the rooting stage.

EARLY-FLOWERING CHRYSANTHEMUMS

TREATMENT OF NEWLY PURCHASED YOUNG PLANTS

In the first season of growing chrysanthemums the amateur will no doubt start by purchasing young rooted plants from chrysanthemum specialists. Treatment depends upon the date of arrival. Young plants received in early May can be planted straight into the prepared open ground where they are to flower. Beginners who have a garden frame are, however, strongly recommended to obtain delivery of rooted plants in mid-March which can be bedded out in the frame 4 inches apart in a layer of John Innes Compost No. 2, and gradually hardened off before transferring them to the open ground. Thereafter the plants should be treated as advised later.

PROPAGATION

Chrysanthemum plants give the best results when they are propagated from cuttings obtained from a post-flowered stool. (See Fig. 5.)

Chrysanthemums, like most other plants, vary from one to another in the vigour of growth and in the quality and form of the flowers ultimately produced. This variation can also apply to individual plants of the same cultivar. It is, therefore, essential for the successful cultivation of chrysanthemums, with the object of obtaining good quality blooms, that we propagate only from the best stock. Stock selection commences during the growing season of the plants, as it will be found that some plants grow and develop more vigorously than others, producing flowers of good form and quality. It is from these plants that the amateur should propagate in the following season.

After flowering, the plants of outdoor cultivars should be cut down to about six inches from the soil and all sappy growth and large leaves removed. (See Fig. 6.) The selected stools should be dug up in early November, the soil shaken off, and the stools dipped in a bucket of insecticide. They can then be planted in frames or packed in trays which should be about 4 in. deep, using J.I. Compost No. 1, or a mixture of half peat and half sand. The trays should be placed in a cold frame or cold

19

Fig. 5. Post-flowered stool dug up in early November

Fig. 6. Post-flowered stool with all growth and large leaves removed

greenhouse, kept cool but free from frost. (See Fig. 7.) Stools overwintered in a cold frame must be given protection when frosts are forecast, by covering the lights with hessian.

It is most important that the compost should not be too wet as stools boxed up into wet compost often rot. Each stool should be carefully labelled with the name of the cultivar.

Six to seven weeks before cuttings are required, transfer the trays of stools to a cold greenhouse and place on the staging. An air temperature of 40–45°F (4–7°C) in the greenhouse at this stage will be satisfactory, but it will be advantageous to provide bottom heat giving a temperature of 60–65°F (15–17°C) to start the stools into vegetative growth.

TAKING CUTTINGS

The best periods for taking cuttings of early-flowering cultivars are from mid-February to the end of March. Readers who wish to time their plants to produce blooms for a particular show date will find from experience (or from information given in the National Chrysanthemum Society's publication *Chrysanthemum Stopping and Timing*) a more definite date in accordance with local conditions.

Cuttings are best rooted on the greenhouse staging with bottom heat, but a cold greenhouse or cold frame may be utilised provided the frost can be kept away from the cuttings. Where heat is not available rooting will, of course, take longer. Stools can be started into active growth in a cold frame in order to obtain cuttings by mid-February, if a plastic soil heating cable is installed in the bed.

Cuttings obtained from the growths appearing at the base of the old stools are preferable to those produced on the stems, although in the case of cultivars which fail to make sufficient basal growths there is no option but to take stem cuttings. The type of cuttings which will make the best plants are those of moderate thickness, wiry and not soft. Large thick cuttings seldom make good plants. A suitable cutting should be about $1\frac{1}{2}$–2 in. in length and should be cleanly cut just below a joint. It is not necessary

Fig. 7. Stools packed in trays and placed in cold greenhouse

to remove any of the lower leaves as cuttings will root quite satisfactorily in this way and this method also produces plants with leaves right down to the base of the stem.

Cuttings may be inserted in seed trays 2 in. deep, or around the edge of $3\frac{1}{2}$ in. pots. There is a choice of composts for rooting chrysanthemum cuttings:

1. The standard John Innes Potting Compost No. 1, detailed on p. 15.
2. Soilless compost, used in accordance with the manufacturer's instructions.
3. A mixture of one part loam, one part peat, and one part sand.

After the compost has been made moderately firm in the seed trays or small pots, it should be covered with a thin layer of sharp sand so that when the holes are made to insert the cuttings, some of the sand will fall to the bottom, upon which the base of the cutting should rest. (See Fig. 8.) A short piece of bamboo cane about $\frac{1}{4}$ in. in diameter can be used for making the holes. Alternatively a pegboard can be made up. (See Fig. 9.)

Fig. 8.   Essentials for rooting procedure – showing suitable cuttings $1\frac{1}{2}$–2 in. in length; seed tray with a layer of sand on top; weak solution of insecticide and hormone rooting powder

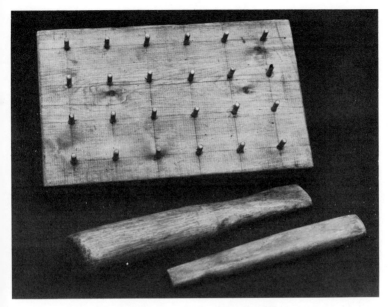

Fig. 9.   Useful gadgets for the amateur – pegboard for making holes in compost to receive cuttings; large pot rammer, and potting stick

To ensure that the cutting is clean and free from pests, it should be dipped in a weak solution of insecticide made up to half the strength recommended by the manufacturers. Shake off the surplus moisture before insertion into the seed tray or small pot.

Cuttings will root easily without artificial aid, but quicker rooting and a much larger root system can be secured by the use of hormone preparations. Powder forms of hormone should be used into which the base of the cutting can be dipped to a depth of $\frac{1}{2}$ in. immediately before insertion.

After the compost around the cuttings has been made firm, it is essential to give a thorough watering using a fine rose on the can. If the compost has been made correctly and gives adequate drainage, a light watering daily can be given to keep the cuttings turgid until rooted. The trays of cuttings will not require any overhead covering if this method is used.

The time of rooting will depend upon the accommodation available to

Fig. 10.   Tray of cuttings showing root development 3–4 weeks after insertion

the grower. If the seed trays of cuttings can be placed on greenhouse staging with bottom heat, rooting will usually take from two to three weeks, although some cultivars will root much more readily than others. An air temperature of about 45–50°F (7–10°C) is very satisfactory. Shading may be necessary on very bright days. (See Fig. 10.)

Trays of cuttings placed on the staging in the greenhouse with bottom heat will cause roots to form quickly and as soon as they appear to be established and begin to grow, they should be moved to cooler quarters in an un-heated greenhouse or, preferably, into a cold frame. When the newly rooted cuttings have become accustomed to the cooler temperature, they should be transplanted before they become long and drawn. They may be planted in the soil of the frame; re-boxed into trays and given more room (12 plants to a tray measuring 16 in. x 12 in. x 4 in.); or they may be potted separately into 3 in. pots.

Rooted cuttings develop well when transplanted into beds in the frame where they are able to grow into strong healthy plants. A frame may be prepared by spreading some ashes on the bottom to a depth of 6 in. The ashes (small cinders and not fine ash) should be well firmed, then covered with a 3 in. layer of the standard John Innes No. 2 compost. The young plants should be placed 4 in. apart in the beds, giving them room to develop into strong plants. The hard ash base keeps the roots compact and they can be lifted easily at planting out time with a 4 in. square of compost attached and very little damage to the roots will be caused.

After planting, the frame should be kept closed for a few days to encourage root action. A light spray with water should be given and a reasonable watering after fourteen days. The aim from now onwards should be to grow the plants under cool and airy conditions, whether they are in the bed of the frame, in trays or pots, and so encourage strong sturdy growth. The plants should on no account be coddled, but great care should be taken to avoid over-watering. The frame lights should be raised and the plants given gradually increasing amounts of air until towards the end of April. The lights can then be left off but turned on if necessary for short periods to protect the plants from either heavy rain or sharp night frosts.

Readers who adopt the pot method for growing on their young plants will find that cuttings which were transplanted into 3 in. pots will need to be potted on into 5 in. early in April. If left in the 3 in. pots they would become pot bound before planting time and roots which have become tightly bound together in a small pot will not develop satisfactorily after planting. Furthermore, the stems become hard and this encourages pre-mature budding. We need at this stage to keep our plants in good vegetative growth, which is prevented by root restriction. Observations made when stools are lifted in the autumn show that plants put out in a pot bound condition still have the closely woven ball of roots intact and a new root system has been developed, causing a serious check to the development of the plant at a time when we need steady growth.

Plants will need a larger pot about six weeks after planting into the first pots. The move should be made when the roots are showing freely around the outside of the ball of compost.

When transferring from 3 in. to 5 in. pots, have the compost only just moist; crock the bottom of the pot and place sufficient compost into the bottom to bring the 3 in. ball of compost to within one inch of the top of the pot. The compost recommended for this potting is John Innes No. 3, and it should be just sufficiently moist that it will bind together when squeezed in the hand yet fall apart when lightly touched with the thumb.

From the time at which the plants are put into the cold frame, a regular spraying with insecticide should be commenced and continued until flowering time. It will be found that by keeping the plants clean from this early stage there will be little or no trouble from insects or birds.

PREPARATION OF THE GROUND

Chrysanthemum plants will grow and produce blooms in most types of garden soil and can be planted adjacent to other subjects in the herbaceous border to give an extension of colour in late summer and autumn. Chrysanthemums virtually grow themselves but the degree of excellence obtained is in direct proportion to the growing conditions. The best results will be obtained by providing a bed or area of ground which has been specially prepared for the purpose. Choose an open site where the ground is well drained and not liable to become waterlogged. Chrysanthemums will not do well under trees or high walls which, although giving shelter from the wind, will cause them to grow exceptionally tall and spindly.

The physical structure of the soil is more important than its nutritive content. It should have an adequate supply of crumbs (small aggregates of soil) to provide for healthy root action.

Farmyard manure, if obtainable, can with advantage be dug into the ground during the winter and a dusting of lime added in early spring. Before applying lime, however, make a pH test of the soil as chrysanthemums prefer it to be slightly on the acid side. If the rating is over 6·5 do not add any lime.

When digging, take out a trench one spit deep and incorporate a layer of manure into the bottom of the trench. The next spit should be thrown over at an angle of 45° and this slope should be covered with a thin layer of manure and a little bonemeal. Repeat this procedure throughout the digging of the bed. This will ensure an even distribution of manure throughout the top 9 in. layer of soil and will provide the necessary humus which will serve as a soil conditioner to put the ground in the right condition for growing good quality plants. When digging is completed the ground should be left to settle down until the beginning of April.

At this time attention should be given to bringing at least the top 6 in. of soil into a crumb-like structure, comparable to the compost in which the plants have been growing prior to planting out. The humus incorporated into the bed when digging, frost, wind and rain will help to create the desired crumb structure of the soil. The grower can also help from early April until planting time by regularly raking down the beds and making them nicely firm.

About two to three weeks prior to planting, the beds should be given a dressing of a balanced chrysanthemum fertilizer at 4–6 oz to the square yard lightly raked into the top of the soil.

When in a dryish and friable condition, the soil in the bed should be pressed down with the feet until it is quite firm. This action will press the soil crumbs closely together to ensure steady but dense root development when the young plants are bedded out.

Those whose aim is to produce top quality blooms for exhibition purposes are advised to have an analysis made of the soil in the chrysanthemum bed, especially if they have been growing chrysanthemums on the same site for several years. It is possible to build up in the soil an excess of chemical salts by a fixed and regular feeding routine using compound fertilizers, which can cause a deterioration in the quality of plants and blooms. The soil analyist will advise the steps to correct such excesses or even maybe deficiencies in the soil. It is most important to know exactly what is in the soil before other chemicals are added. Those who have taken the advice of a soil analyst have found a great improvement in the health and vigour of their plants.

PLANTING OUT

Experience has shown that the best time for planting in the open ground in the south of England is the second week of May, provided this does not coincide with either a very wet period or a late frosty spell. If either of these contingencies arise at this time, planting out should be deferred until weather conditions are more favourable. In the north of England planting out should generally be deferred until the end of the month, according to the known climatic conditions of the area.

If it is possible to have special beds for Early-flowering Chrysanthemums, they should be planted in beds of three rows, 15 in. between plants and 15 in. between rows, with a path 30 in. wide between the beds. The pathways make easy access to the plants for summer treatment.

A good trowel is essential for making the hole to receive the plant—the stainless steel tool is ideal for this purpose. With a little practice a hole can be made into which the plant will fit snugly. It is important to see that the ground around the plant is made firm after planting so that there are no air pockets underneath the plant. The importance of growing chrysanthemums in firm ground has already been stressed.

If a basin or hollow 2 in. deep is left around each plant, this will facilitate early watering and give the plants some protection from wind in the early stages. The depression will become filled with the surrounding soil when the beds are hoed later.

STAKING

It is desirable that the plants should be staked and tied at an early date to prevent wind damage. Bamboo canes 3 ft long are preferred by many growers to 4 ft canes, as long canes frequently give rise to damage of the blooms later in the season as they get bruised by rubbing on the upper portion of the cane in windy weather. It is recommended that the canes should be placed in position at planting time, and after each plant is in position it should be carefully tied to the cane provided, having the first tie $1\frac{1}{2}$ to 2 in. from ground level as a support against wind strain.

SUMMER WORK

In the early part of the season the ground around the growing plants should be frequently hoed and kept clear of weeds. A fine tilth should be maintained and the soil should not be allowed to become hard on the surface. When using the hoe, it should be kept very shallow, not more than half an inch into the soil.

The maintenance of this fine tilth on the surface of the bed retains the moisture underneath, thus enabling the plant to grow freely. Some watering may be necessary in these early stages to ensure that the plants get away quickly and do not stand still for any appreciable length of time. Ten days standstill at this period will make a great deal of difference at the end of the season.

Small quantities of nitrogen in the form of dried blood or sulphate of ammonia can safely be used at this time to assist plants that appear to be at a standstill.

The soil must not be allowed to become hard and caked. If the ground has been hoed regularly and a 2 in. tilth of loose soil maintained around the plants, there should be little need for watering. In a drought, when it is necessary to water, each plant should be given a thorough soaking. It is of little use just damping the upper half an inch of soil.

Regularly spraying with insecticide should be continued, and after hot days the plants will much appreciate an overhead spray with clear water.

Chrysanthemums are not deep rooting plants and during July they develop roots just below the surface of the soil. Although the hoe is the gardener's best friend, this tool must not be used around chrysanthemum plants from mid-July onwards as it is important that the newly formed roots should not be damaged.

STOPPING

It is often found that the most baffling aspect of chrysanthemum growing to the beginner is the subject of *Stopping*. With well grown plants there should be little or no difficulty for the amateur who wants a good display in his garden. It is sufficient to know whether or not a plant needs to be

Fig. 11. Stopping – the removal of the growing point of the plant

stopped to encourage breaks from the leaf axils which will develop and produce flowers before the autumn frosts. It is always preferable that plants develop naturally and that our cultivation methods only assist nature in its work.

Stopping is the removal of the growing point on the main stem of the plant. By removing this tip before a bud appears, lateral growths will develop sooner than if the plant was allowed to grow and break naturally.

Early-flowering Chrysanthemums, almost without exception, give the best blooms when they are allowed to flower on First Crown buds. All cultivars will break naturally and there are some which, when left to break naturally, will produce fully developed blooms during September and early October. Other cultivars must be stopped to encourage earlier breaks and to give sufficient time for the lateral growths to develop and form flower buds which will mature before the autumn frosts.

Plants must be in the right condition at stopping time. They should have a well developed root system and be in vigorous vegetative growth. If the reader has followed the cultural advice given, plants should be in this condition about the 25th May.

To stop a plant, approximately a quarter of an inch of the growing point of the stem should be removed to retain the maximum amount of soft growth, as this is the type of material that will produce plenty of breaks. (See Fig. 11.) If too much of the tip is removed, breaks will be reluctant to emerge from the lower and hard part of the stems. Plants thus treated will quickly respond by sending out lateral growths from the leaf axils.

The act of stopping will not by itself induce a bigger or better plant. Backward plants will not be all that hastened by the operation, neither will the growth of very poor plants be very much assisted. It must be stressed that the plants must be in the right condition.

Plants that are ready for stopping should have the breaks in embryo form at the axils. It is essential after stopping to stimulate the production of stem and breaks and a nitrogenous fertilizer in the form of a liquid top dressing will fulfil the need. Dissolve one ounce of sulphate of ammonia in one gallon of water and apply this quantity to $1\frac{1}{4}$ sq. yds of soil.

To obtain good quality blooms, not more than six lateral growths should be allowed to grow; the others should be cut out at an early date. If the plants are being grown for garden decoration, eight or nine breaks may be allowed to develop to give a good display of smaller sized blooms.

Some six or seven weeks after the laterals have started to grow, there will appear at the end of these shoots a First Crown bud. This bud should be secured by removing all other buds and shoots which may appear in the leaf axils all the way down the stem. It will be found that as a general rule it will take from six to eight weeks from the time of securing the bud to having the bloom fully open. It should be possible to secure the First Crown bud between the middle and the end of July, and the buds of practically all early-flowering cultivars should have been secured by the end of the first week of August.

As the breaks develop, they should be supported by loops of garden twine to the bamboo cane (provided to support the plant when bedded out) in order to prevent them breaking off when exposed to strong winds which often occur during the latter part of the summer.

Should the reader be growing chrysanthemums for exhibition purposes, he is advised to reduce the number of lateral growths to three per plant and to provide a separate cane for each lateral.

An individual support for each stem will be necessary as the fully matured blooms will be up to 7 in. in diameter. The canes should be inserted into the ground at an angle inclining away from the plant, and each stem is then tied to a separate cane so that it cannot be blown about by the wind and thus damage the blooms.

Counting down the lateral growths to the desired number of three or four should not be carried out in one operation. Reduce them gradually over a period for the following reasons:-

1. To maintain the balanced growth of the plant.
2. To prevent hard centres (too many florets in the centre of the bloom unable to unfurl and develop satisfactorily).
3. There is always the risk of a lateral growth being broken or damaged by gale force winds, storm damage, birds or pests.

The final count-down to three or four breaks per plant should coincide with the securing of the bud. At this period of the plant's development the number of florets in each bloom will have been predetermined. Reducing the number of stems after the buds have been secured will help to increase petal size, both in length and breadth, to produce the larger bloom required by the exhibitor.

TWO LEAF STOP

Certain cultivars may only produce three lateral growths per plant. If this should occur, reduce each of the three laterals back to the lower pair of leaves on each break. Usually two further breaks will emerge from the leaf axils on each stem, to give six breaks where only three main flowering shoots per plant existed before.

PREMATURE BUDS

If we have a hot dry season in May or June, the stems of Early-flowering Chrysanthemums in the open will ripen and become hard and brittle, and some plants will develop premature buds. Here the two leaf stop can be applied and is often effective.

If fresh young growth is not sent out from these leaf axils, strong suckers will grow up very quickly from the base of the plant and one bud should be allowed to develop at the end of each sucker. Blooms produced in this way are usually quite satisfactory.

FEEDING

If the chrysanthemum bed has been properly prepared, supplementary feeding should not be necessary as there should be sufficient plant food available in the soil to produce good quality blooms. Good cultivation builds up a plant that is in the balance, having a well developed root system and producing sturdy healthy plant growth that will give good quality blooms. Frequent applications of fertilizer can make the root system sick and lazy. Providing the soil structure is right, the roots will penetrate into the soil and take up the plant foods required. There should be ample available if the ground has been prepared in accordance with the recommendations given.

On light sandy soils, where the plant foods can be leached away by heavy rains, two dressings of a well balanced chrysanthemum fertilizer should be applied, one in mid-June and the other in mid-July; at the rate of 2–4 oz per square yard. During dry weather, water the soil before and after application.

SECURING THE BUD

With regard to the dates when buds become visible on early-flowering cultivars, this will depend to a great extent on the weather experienced during the growing season rather than on the length of day. In a season when we have a reasonable amount of moist warm weather, numerous early-flowering cultivars will be in full bud by the 15th July and many can be completely disbudded by the 22nd July in the south of England. It should be noted that at this time of year the sun rises at about 4 a.m. and sets at about 8.15 p.m.—that is, about 17 hours of daylight, allowing for a short period before sunrise and after sunset.

The statement frequently made to the effect that chrysanthemums need a short day of about ten hours of daylight in order to develop buds, does not therefore apply to the early-flowering types. Most growers in the south of England should be able to have all their Early-flowering Chrysanthemums fully disbudded by the 15th August, thus allowing a period of six weeks for them to develop their best blooms before the end of September.

THE FINAL STAGES

By early August the buds on most of the cultivars will have been secured, leaving six or seven weeks of waiting before the flowers reach maturity. During this period there is often a renewed growth of side shoots from the leaf axils and suckers from the base of the plant, which should be removed to direct all the plant's energy to the developing buds. With the development of the flowers, plants become slightly top heavy and it is advisable to check over the supporting canes, looking for any which may have rotted at ground level.

Suckers will appear in mid-September and these can be left to develop masses of small sprays in October.

Pests can still be troublesome—capsids, greenfly and earwigs will spoil a promising flower. The routine spray of Malathion will take care of greenfly and capsids, and a dusting with DDT powder will control earwigs.

There are a few cultivars susceptible to mildew and this will show itself firstly on the underside of the leaves. One or two sprays with Karathane will clear up this trouble and prevent it from spreading. (See Chap. 7).

PROTECTION FROM WEATHER DAMAGE

Most of the modern Early-flowering disbudded chrysanthemums are fairly weatherproof when grown to produce six to seven blooms per plant for garden display or floral arrangement, and will not require any overhead protection whatsoever at flowering time.

Those who grow their plants for show purposes will restrict the number of blooms to two, three or four per plant and such blooms will be six or seven inches in diameter with appropriate depth of bloom. Flowers of this size are very liable to damage by wind and rain if storms occur at the time when the blooms are well developed. The keen exhibitor cannot afford to take the risk of storm damage to the opening flower during the three weeks before it reaches the peak of perfection. Some of the blooms would no doubt develop satisfactorily without protection and, even if inclement weather was experienced, would sustain only minor damage that would pass unnoticed by the general public, but for the exhibitor this is not good enough.

Minor damage and blemishes would not escape the eagle eye of the chrysanthemum judge. Exhibitors have tried many schemes during the last few years with the object of being able to place on the show bench perfect blooms without spot or blemish of any kind.

Many exhibitors have taken to the use of paper bags for protection of blooms of large-flowered early cultivars grown in the open ground. The experience of many successful exhibitors proves that the ordinary grease-proof paper bag gives the best results if used in the proper way. They are just sufficiently porous to absorb the moisture transpired by the flower.

The bags must be absolutely airtight and sealed with waterproof glue so that the seal does not come apart and let the bag split open when it gets very wet. The best quality greasproof bag size 10 in. will suit most cultivars. The 12 in. size will be needed for extra large cultivars.

A double bag—that is, one bag placed inside another, will stand up to the worst weather. After a period of heavy rain the water may percolate through the outer bag and be trapped between it and the inner bag. The weight of the trapped water can bend the neck and possibly break the flower head off—unless precautions are taken. To prevent this damage

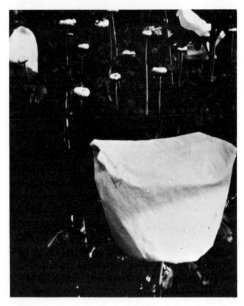

Fig. 12. *Buds showing colour and ready for bagging. Bag placed over bud and tied to stem*

occurring, the outside bag should be punctured all round with small holes approximately three inches from the bottom. The holes will then be in the proper position for draining off any trapped water. Thus we have the airtight inner bag giving rigidity and shape and the punctured outer bag holding off the main weight of rain and draining off the surplus.

Bags can be prepared in advance. The airtight inner bag can be placed inside the punctured bag before the start of the actual work of covering the buds. The buds showing colour should have been sprayed previously to kill any greenfly, and then allowed to dry. Buds must not be bagged when they are wet.

First, test the stem 'neck' under the bud for strength. If it is 'rubbery' leave for a few days, by which time the neck will have become rigid and strong. Most of the blooms showing colour will have necks strong enough to bear the weight of the bags, although if attempts are made to bag buds before the colour shows, practically all buds will be found to have rubbery necks.

Dip the bottom half-inch of the mouth of the bag in a pail of water to soften the tough greaseproof paper, thus helping the bottom tie to be made more easily and tightly. Flatten out the top corners of the bag, blow up the bag like a toy balloon, and place it over the bud aiming to cover two inches of the stem directly under the bag for tying. Press and shape the bottom two inches of the bag to the stem until it will cling unheld to the stem. After this pressing, the half-inch of wet bag will have spread to make one inch of pliable paper for the bottom tie, which should be applied first. It is preferable to make more than one tie to ensure that there is no risk of the bag becoming detached from the stem.

When the double bag is firmly tied on, place the left hand under the bag and support as you press down the top of the bag to give the desired shape for the petals to develop. Double bags cause the pink and red cultivars to lose colour, but yellow and white cultivars are not affected as regards colour. (See Fig. 12.)

When taking the bags off fully developed blooms, a stroke with a safety razor blade will cut through the string holding the bag in position. No attempt should be made to remove the bag whole as great damage may be caused to the bloom. The bag should be carefully torn off to release the bloom and the florets will then quickly re-arrange themselves after the stems have had an hour or so in a vase or bucket of water.

In addition to protecting the blooms from weather damage, exhibitors will find that the paper bag does help to give a better finish to incurved blooms. Experience has shown that when inside the paper bag the top florets are drawn more closely together, giving a completely globular finish to the flower, without an opening in the centre which is a fault when blooms of this type are shown for exhibition purposes.

4. EARLY-FLOWERING SPRAY CULTIVARS, INCLUDING POMPON TYPES

These are other sections of the chrysanthemum most suitable for garden display and floral arrangement.

Sprays are very floriferous—each plant will produce from six to ten branches each carrying clusters of well-formed chrysanthemums varying in size from 1 to 2 in. in diameter according to the cultivar.

Some well grown Pompons will produce hundreds of flowers on compact bushy plants. In addition to this abundance, flowering is maintained over a long period from the end of July until mid-October.

The basic principles of cultivation are in general the same as those advised for disbudded cultivars: Post-flowered stools are lifted and boxed up during November and overwintered in the cold frame and greenhouse; cuttings are inserted in seed trays at the end of February.

During mid-May, plants are taken from the cold frame and transplanted about 15 in. apart each way into beds in the garden. The plants should be supported by short canes as a protection against wind damage.

To encourage the early development of a good plant structure, give frequent overhead dampings in the evenings after dry days in June.

In general terms it is not considered necessary to stop the plants, but to assist them to develop their branching habit, as the break bud appears on each plant it should be removed. During June all buds that are visible should be removed. Only remove the bud, do not take off any part of the stem. This will allow the breaks to multiply and greatly increase the number of flowering stems and the ultimate size of the plant. If the buds that appeared in June were left to flower, this would retard the growth of the plant and considerably reduce its ultimate size and flower production.

From mid-July onwards, allow the flower buds to develop. At this time the plant will have developed many branches which will continue in bloom until early October. As the individual flowers fade, they should be removed to encourage further plant growth.

5. OCTOBER, MID-SEASON AND LATE-FLOWERING CHRYSANTHEMUMS

CULTIVATION OF OCTOBER-FLOWERING CHRYSANTHEMUMS

To fill the period of time between the end of the Early flowering Chrysanthemum season until the Mid-season types commence blooming, we have the October-flowering Chrysanthemums. Within this group there are many very attractive flowers. The shorter day length and cooler conditions usually prevailing at this period produces blooms which are more intense in colour.

The grower has a choice of methods for their cultivation. October-flowering Chrysanthemums may be grown and flowered quite successfully in the open garden, depending on local climatic conditions. In the south of England there should be no problem as severe frosts are seldom experienced during the first weeks of October. Some form of overhead protection will be sufficient to protect the developing blooms from inclement weather. This can be provided by making up light wooden frames which are covered with a heavy gauge clear polythene and erected over the plants.

The general cultural routine should be the same as given for Early-flowering Chrysanthemums. In areas where the weather conditions deteriorate rapidly during October, the plants should be grown in 8 or 9 in. pots, as recommended for the Mid-season and Late-flowering Chrysanthemums, and given greenhouse protection at flowering time.

CULTIVATION OF MID-SEASON AND LATE-FLOWERING CHRYSANTHEMUMS

For those who wish to progress to the Mid-season and Late-flowering sections, the essential requirement will be to possess a greenhouse into which the pots containing the well-developed chrysanthemum plants can be transferred at the end of September.

Many amateur gardeners use their greenhouses to raise seedlings in the Spring and to grow tomato plants during the Summer. The chrysanthemum is a suitable subject to follow on after the tomato crop has been harvested and will provide a continuation of flowers until the end of December.

Those who have enjoyed the pleasure of growing Early-flowering Chrysanthemums in the open garden will find the Mid-season and Late-flowering types most rewarding.

One of the greatest pleasures of growing the Late-flowering types of chrysanthemum is to be able to enter one's greenhouse on a dull winter day to be greeted with a display of blooms of varying shades of colour and form—the end product of a most rewarding hobby.

In the early stages, the cultivation methods are the same as those given for Early-flowering Chrysanthemums, with the following exceptions:

1. The date of rooting the cuttings commences at the end of December proceeding through January, February and March, according to the type being grown—Large and Medium Exhibition, Incurved, Decorative, Singles or Sprays.

2. After rooting, all plants must go through a succession of pots, gradually increasing in size—first 3 in., then 5 in., and finally 8–10 in., in order to build up a large root system. Good quality blooms cannot be obtained by cutting out intermediate stages by potting small plants immediately into large sized pots. The compost to be used at each successive stage of potting should be gradually richer.

Commercial cut flower growers of today do not usually grow and flower chrysanthemums in large pots. After rooting they are directly planted into prepared beds in greenhouses. As this book has been written specifically for amateur growers, the cultivation methods given are those that have been practised with great success by leading amateurs for many years.

WINTER CARE OF STOOLS

Stools of cultivars that have flowered in pots in the greenhouse need not be disturbed. Cut down the flowering stems to 6–9 in. from soil level, remove all green growth, and place the pots in a position where the stools can obtain plenty of light and air.

With regard to temperature, it has been established that some cultivars require a period of vernalisation if they are to grow satisfactorily in the following year. This vernalisation requirement will be fulfilled if the stools are kept for a period of about three weeks in a cool greenhouse at a night temperature of not more than 40°F (4°C).

POTTING PROCEDURE

The routine procedure for first, second and final potting is the same for all sections of the Mid-season and Late-flowering type; the only variation is in the size of the final pot.

First Potting

Cuttings of the Large Exhibition section taken in December or January, if kept in a heated greenhouse at 50°F (10°C), should be nicely rooted by early February and ready for the first potting. The standard John Innes potting compost No. 2, and 3 in. pots can be used. As soon as the young plants have recovered from the move and are established in the small pots (say ten days after potting), they should be transferred to cooler quarters in a cold frame. The plants should be allowed room to develop and should not be overcrowded. Open the frame lights on all suitable occasions but ensure that the young plants do not become frozen. Water should be given only when really necessary. It is essential to keep the compost on the dry side as this encourages root development and avoids spindly growth.

The plants should be sprayed occasionally with a suitable insecticide to keep them clear of aphids. If low-pressure aerosols are used instead of liquid sprays, great care must be taken to ensure that the jet of insecticide from the aerosol does not touch the foliage of the young plants. The solvent used in the aerosols will burn the foliage.

Fig. 13.   Plant from a 3-inch pot showing root development prior to being potted on into a 5-inch pot

Second Potting

Do not allow the plants to remain in the 3 in. pots until they become pot-bound, with the roots entwined round and round the tiny ball of soil. (See Fig. 13.) On the other hand, do not re-pot them until the roots have taken full hold of the compost—as soon as this stage is reached the plants must be transferred to 5 in. pots. This move should normally be made between the middle and end of March, although too much importance should not be attached to the date. The emphasis must be on the full root development in the smaller pot. J.I.P.3 compost can be used at this stage.

The compost should be compacted moderately firm using a potting stick. (See Fig. 9.) Insert a short split cane about 18 in. in length to support the plant against wind damage.

Final Potting

The Compost

The plants will be in this compost for the rest of their lives; and it is essential that this final potting is carried out with great care. First, ensure that the loam used is suitable for the purpose. It should have an adequate crumb structure as loam in this condition will provide for healthy root action. The clay content should be such as to leave a greasy smear when rubbed on the hand. Small fibres should also be in evidence, indicating that the loam has come from the top spit of grassland. The sand in the final potting compost should be in the form of grit $\frac{1}{8}$ to $\frac{3}{16}$ maximum size and dust free. Cornish grit is an ideal material.

After the ingredients of the compost have been well mixed together, they should be left for two weeks to mature and sweeten before being used for potting. Keep the rain and sun off the mixture and turn it over once or twice in the meantime.

Before commencing to use the compost, ensure that the moisture content is correct. It should be just sufficiently moist that it will bind together when squeezed in the hand yet fall apart when lightly touched with the thumb.

The Method

From the middle to the end of May, the plants should be ready for transfer to the final pots, and here again the move should not be made until the full root development has been reached in the smaller pot. A compost made up to the J.I.P. 4 formula will be satisfactory for the final potting.

Traditional clay pots are still extensively used by amateurs. Plastic pots are also satisfactory, although composts do not dry out so quickly in this type of pot—an advantage during hot dry spells but presenting the opposite

Fig. 14.   5-inch pot used as a mould during final potting procedure

Fig. 15.   Compost being firmed round the mould with a rammer

Fig. 16.   Mould removed. The large pot is now ready to receive the plant taken from its 5-inch pot

problem during very wet weather. My choice would always be a clay pot. The size of pot will be either 9 or 10 in. according to the vigour of the plant.

First, place some crocks in the bottom of the pot to ensure good drainage. (See Fig. 14). Cover the crocks with some fibrous pieces of loam. Compact down firmly using a rammer. (See Fig. 9.)

Have to hand a 5 in. pot to be used as a mould, and place this inside the larger pot. Place sufficient compost under the 5 in. pot to bring it up to within $1\frac{1}{2}$ in. from the top of the larger pot. (See Fig. 14.)

At this stage place about a $\frac{1}{4}$ in. layer of peat underneath the mould to retain moisture and keep the roots cool during hot weather. With the mould in position then proceed to gradually fill up the surrounding space with your prepared compost, using the rammer at intervals to ensure firmness until the compost is level with the rim of the mould. (Fig. 15.) The compost should be so firmly rammed that it will not indent when pressed with the fingers. The mould can then be removed and the plant to be potted on should then be placed in position. (Fig. 16.) There will be a small space, the thickness of the pot between the ball of soil and the wall of compost in the larger pot. A further ramming will compact this close to the soil ball.

It can readily be seen that by using this method there is no risk whatsoever of damaging the roots when ramming the soil round the smaller ball of soil. Now is the time to insert a stout bamboo cane $\frac{1}{2}$ in.–$\frac{5}{8}$ in. in diameter and 4–5 ft in length, according to the known height of the cultivar, to provide support for the plant.

When the final potting is complete, the plants should be placed 'pot thick' in a shady part of the garden and no water given to them on any account for at least ten to fourteen days. (Fig. 17.) Providing the plants were watered before potting, and that the moisture content of the compost was correct, only an occasional overhead spray with a fine rosed can is necessary. This will encourage the root systems to go out and find their own water and a vigorous root system will be built up.

Soilless Composts

Amateurs who choose to grow pot chrysanthemums in soilless compost must follow the instructions given by the manufacturers with regard to firming the compost when potting on into final pots.

Leave a 2 in. space at the top of the pot for top dressing, feeding and watering. Usually plants in soilless compost will require feeding more frequently as the buffering effect of peat is not the same as with loam based composts. However, amateur growers have grown very good quality blooms using peat based soilless composts as the growing medium.

Fig. 17. Plants in final pots standing 'pot thick' in a shady part of the garden

STOPPING AND TIMING

When grown under natural conditions, each type of chrysanthemum has an inbred characteristic to flower at an approximate time to produce blooms of the maximum potential for the particular cultivar. Any attempt by the grower to alter the flowering date considerably by stopping at an earlier or later date than recommended will usually result in blooms of inferior quality.

The date when cuttings are rooted is equally important. Some cultivars in the Large Exhibition section can be left to break naturally, and this usually occurs at the end of May or early June. From then until their flowering time during November there is sufficient time for the laterals to grow and produce their buds. (See Figs. 18 and 19).

For those needing to be stopped, as a general guide cuttings should be rooted 14–16 weeks ahead of the recommended stopping date.

Experience over many years has shown that in Britain Large Exhibition cultivars produce the finest flowers in November from buds secured between the 7th and 20th August. If buds which appear in mid-July are secured, they seldom open satisfactorily.

The object of stopping Large Exhibition cultivars is to assist the plant to produce buds that can be secured at the best time—namely mid-August. It is usual to aim at obtaining two blooms per plant.

Amateurs should start with *Natural break* cultivars. These are types which, when cuttings have been rooted in January, will break naturally during May—that is, they will send out side growths of their own accord without any stopping. Many lateral growths may be sent out from the main stem at the time when the natural break occurs, but only two should be retained and allowed to grow. All the other side growths should be removed. If this is carried out, the plant will produce a First Crown bud at the end of each of the two remaining laterals at the correct time in mid-August.

If, by any chance, any Natural break cultivars have not made a natural break by the last week of May, they must be stopped once by removing just the tip of the main stem. The plant will then send out side growths. Only two of these should be allowed to grow and the plant should be treated just as if it had made a natural break.

(See National Chrysanthemum Society publication *Chrysanthemum Stopping and Timing* for a list of cultivars and their stopping dates.)

Fig. 18.   Plant ready for stopping
14–16 weeks after rooting. Note balanced
and short-jointed growth

Fig. 19.   Effect of stopping – strong
lateral growths developing from leaf
axils

Fig. 20.   Plants in their summer quarters supported by canes secured to cross-wires

SUMMER QUARTERS

Two weeks after the final potting the plants should be transferred to their summer quarters, usually referred to as the 'standing-out ground'. Choose an open site in the garden away from trees or high walls. Chrysanthemums will appreciate all the sunshine available throughout the summer months.

If possible, provide an ash base 3 in. thick on which to stand the pots or, alternatively, they can be placed on boards. The object of this is to prevent worms entering the pots through the drainage holes and the risk of pots standing on a waterlogged site after heavy summer rains.

Place the pots in rows, leaving as much distance as possible between the rows, allowing room for the wielding of a watering can and detailed inspection of the plants. There should be a spacing of at least 9 in. between each pot.

Some additional support will be required to prevent the pots from being blown over during strong winds. It is advisable to put up a framework to which the canes supporting the plants can be tied. Stout end posts should be driven into the ground at each end of the rows and two or three wires strained between them. (See Fig. 20.) If considered necessary, lighter intermediary supports can be inserted, and the end posts in their turn secured by a guy wire attached to a good peg driven into the ground at an acute angle.

If each cane is tied to these cross wires as soon as the plants are put out in position, there need be little fear of the worst of weather conditions.

Whilst in their summer quarters, the plants should be regularly sprayed at approximately 14-day intervals with an insecticide to ensure that the plants, and particularly the growing points, are kept free from pest attack. Prevention is better than cure.

When warm humid conditions prevail during July, some cultivars will be susceptible to mildew and this will show itself firstly on the underside of the leaves. One or two sprays with Karathane will clear up this trouble and prevent it from spreading.

FEEDING

Feeding plays an important part in the cultivation routine of pot plants, although many growers mistakenly believe that it is the beginning and the end of chrysanthemum growing and that within the feeding programme lies the whole secret of growing.

The compost used for final potting will contain sufficient plant foods to maintain a balanced growth for approximately one month. During that time the developing roots will have absorbed the available plant food while a certain amount will have been leached away when watering the plants.

Little and often should be the rule when feeding. Some five weeks after final potting, commence a routine feed giving half a teaspoonful of a balanced chrysanthemum fertilizer to each plant every seven days. It should be spread evenly over the soil surface and lightly watered in. Continue feeding in this way until the flower buds begin to show colour.

When completing the final potting, the soil level was $1\frac{1}{2}$–2 in. below the rim of the pot, allowing space for top dressings of compost as the plant develops and makes roots near to the surface. Have available some final potting compost and apply quarter inch layers every two weeks, commencing six to seven weeks after final potting, and continue until the soil level is only 1 in. below the rim of the pot to allow for watering.

By this means a steady and balanced growth will continue until flowering time.

WATERING

Experienced chrysanthemum growers will know without any doubt whatsoever that the most important task in the cultivation of their plants is what is often referred to as 'the art of watering'. Correct watering will ensure the build up of firm ripe wood essential for the production of good quality flowers. This cannot be carried out with a daily dose from the hosepipe!

Plants should never be given water until they need it. An excess of water will restrict growth and root development. Healthy growth is produced by making the roots work and search for moisture.

Some growers will consider that they can tell by the look of a plant whether or not it requires water. On the other hand there are growers of many years experience who always use a little tool known as a 'pot tapper'. This is usually a 'do-it-yourself' job, comprising a piece of cane 30 in. long with a cotton reel attached to one end. Armed with this little gadget and the watering can, proceed along the rows of plants giving each pot a tap. If it rings this will indicate that the compost in the pot is drying out and requires water.

Avoid watering in the evenings if possible as this tends to give an upward surge of sap at the wrong time of the day when transpiration and evaporation are at their lowest. The only water to be applied to the plants in the evening should be a fine light overhead spray after warm days.

SECURING THE BUDS

When the buds appear in mid-August they must be secured. All growths in the leaf axils below the bud should be gradually removed, when they are about three-quarters of an inch long and can be handled safely without damaging the stalk of the flower. If a bud has appeared rather too early, it can be retarded for about a week by allowing some of the lower leaf axil shoots to grow until they are up to 2 in. long. If, however, these delaying tactics are persisted for too long, the bud selected will suffer.

Some experienced growers flower only one bloom per plant. The procedure is to allow two breaks to develop until the buds have been secured, and at this time the best break is retained and the other one removed. This should be carried out gradually by taking off approximately 2 in. of the break each day until it has been completely removed. The advantage of this procedure is as follows: At the time when the buds are secured, the number of florets that will develop in the bloom has been predetermined and removing one break at this late stage will enable the remaining bud to increase its petal size, thus giving a larger bloom when it reaches maturity. Growers must experiment to ascertain which cultivars will respond to this treatment.

HOUSING

For the uninitiated this means transferring the chrysanthemum plants growing in pots from their summer quarters into a greenhouse.

The work should commence as the buds begin to show colour. For the Large Exhibition type this will be around the 20th September.

The greenhouse should be thoroughly cleansed using a disinfectant and also fumigated to destroy all insects and pests before the plants are moved in. There are a number of suitable fumigants available in the form of smoke cones containing Malathion, B.H.C., or Nictone which will be most effective in ensuring a clean start.

Before each plant is taken into the greenhouse, it should be defoliated for approximately 2 ft up the stem to allow for air circulation when the plants are inside. Removal of the lower leaves at this stage of plant development will not have any adverse effect.

The pot should be thoroughly washed, and the whole of the plant sprayed with Malathion (an insecticide) and Karathane (a fungicide). These chemicals are compatible and can be mixed together.

Try to avoid overcrowding the plants in the greenhouse as air circulation around them is most important. When the plants are housed, all ventilators and the door should be kept open for a week or two, then gradually closed down as the weather deteriorates. Endeavour to maintain a temperature of 50°F (10°C).

Frost is not the greatest danger to the developing blooms. The worst enemy is *damping*. A close humid atmosphere on a warm foggy day can cause much more damage than a few degrees of frost at night. The introduction of fan-type heaters for use in large and small greenhouses have proved to be most effective in minimising the risk of damping. A 'still' atmosphere must be avoided at all costs.

Damping is due to the fungus *Botrytis* and in some cases orthocide dust (Captan) has been successfully used as a preventative.

It is always possible for insect pests to enter the greenhouse through the ventilators, and therefore the grower is advised to fumigate at fortnightly intervals after the plants have been housed.

The general cultivation routine outlined applies to Large Exhibition and Medium Exhibition types. When growing Exhibition Incurved, Decorative, Single and Spray types of Mid-season and Late-flowering Chrysanthemums, the cultural routine is the same up to the final potting stage. From then onwards there are specific requirements for each type, and I will deal with these under their respective sections.

ADDITIONAL CULTURAL NOTES FOR EXHIBITION INCURVED, DECORATIVE, SINGLE AND SPRAY TYPES

Exhibition Incurved

An Exhibition Incurved bloom should be as nearly a globe as possible. the florets may be either rounded or pointed at the tips, forming a solid symmetrical bloom of generally globular outline. The lay and density of the florets should be even throughout the bloom and the centre filled to form the top of the sphere. These are considered to be a very classical type of flower and are greatly admired when well grown.

The final pot size should be 8 in. and the compost rammed quite firm, leaving the recommended 2 in. space at the top for top-dressing.

Well-formed globular flowers of the incurved type will be produced on First Crown buds from cuttings taken in January. The plants will normally make a natural break in the south of England in the second week of June. Allow up to six laterals to develop to produce blooms for cut flower and decorative work. Exhibitors should reduce the laterals to three but this should not be carried out until the buds have been secured. The First Crown bud will appear at the end of these lateral growths during early September. It is then secured, and the blooms will reach maturity from November onwards.

For some cultivars it is recommended that they be flowered on Second Crown buds, which means that the lateral growths will have to be stopped twice. Second Crown blooms are usually smaller in size as the second stop has the effect of reducing the number of florets in each bloom, although they are usually more refined in form. The first stopping, about the 15th April, consists of removing just the tip of the main stem of the plant. Following this stopping only three side shoots should be allowed to grow. The others should be removed. The second stopping should take place in the middle of June when the growing point of each of the three lateral growths should be removed. This will cause new shoots to develop in the leaf axils of the three laterals. If it is desired to obtain only three show quality blooms per plant, only one of the new shoots should be allowed to grow on each lateral, all other shoots in the leaf axils of the first breaks being removed. The three new shoots will then grow on until early September when they are about 18 in. long, the Second Crown bud will appear at the end of each of them. These buds should then be secured in the usual way by removing all unwanted growths that develop in the leaf axils below the required bud.

If six or nine blooms are required per plant for cut flower and decorative purposes, two or three shoots, instead of only one, should be allowed to grow from each of the first three breaks after the second stopping.

Reflexed and Intermediate Decoratives

These two sections of Decoratives include a greater number of cultivars than all other Late-flowering sections combined, and are similar in every way to the Early-flowering types grown in the open garden. Their cultivation is fairly simple when compared with the more exacting timing requirements of Large Exhibition types. The amateur, after some experience with Early-flowering cultivars, when first embarking upon the cultivation of Late-flowering cultivars would be well advised to start with Decoratives and master their cultivation before attempting to grow the more difficult Large Exhibition and Exhibition Incurved types.

Cuttings of Decoratives are best taken from mid-January to the end of February. The succession of pots procedure and the compost to be used at the different stages are the same as described for Large Exhibition cultivars. In the case of Decoratives, however, the first potting of the young rooted cuttings into 3 in. pots should not take place until the end of March. The second move should be into 5 in. pots and should normally be carried out about a month after the first potting—dependent upon the progress which the young plants have made in the 3 in. pots. Here again it must be emphasised that the plants should not be allowed to become 'pot bound', but at the same time they must not be moved on into larger pots until the roots have taken full possession of the compost in the smaller pot. The plants should usually be ready for final potting into 8 in. 9 in. or 10 in. pots from mid-May to early June.

If cuttings are taken in January and February, the plants usually produce the best blooms from First Crown buds. There are, however, exceptions to this general rule. 'Princess Anne', for example, is best flowered on Second Crown buds. This procedure has already been described for the Exhibition Incurved types.

Most Decoratives, Reflexed and Intermediate, can be allowed to make a natural break. If this break has not occurred by the 15th June, the growing point of the plant should be removed and up to nine lateral growths allowed to develop.

Amateurs growing for exhibition purposes should allow up to six breaks to grow after the natural break. The number can be reduced still further at the time when the buds are secured in order to produce larger blooms, as previously explained.

In some instances it may be necessary to stop the plants before the 15th June in order to give sufficient time for the lateral growths to form buds that will produce fully developed blooms during the early weeks of November. A study of the National Chrysanthemum Society's publication *Chrysanthemum Stopping and Timing* will give the recommended dates for individual cultivars.

Singles

A Single chrysanthemum has approximately five rows of ray florets with a central disk which gives the appearance of a small cushion, either green or yellow in colour. As well as being an exhibitors flower, Singles are ideal subjects for floral arrangements as they have a light and delicate appearance, particularly when the plants are grown to produce a crop of medium sized flowers.

Single cultivars should be given the same general treatment as already outlined for Decoratives as regards a succession of pots and the use of gradually richer potting composts at the various stages of repotting.

Most Singles give the best flowers on Second Crown buds. If flowered on First Crowns the blooms are frequently semi-double—that is, they have more than the five rows of ray florets. Furthermore, they frequently give flowers with incurving florets instead of flat florets at right angles to the stem.

The first potting of the rooted cuttings into 3 in. pots should be carried out in March, as in the case of Decoratives. The second potting into 5 in. pots should usually be in April—as soon as the roots have taken full hold of the compost in the 3 in. pots.

The first stopping, which consists of removing the growing tip of the main stem, should be undertaken about the middle of April when the Singles are in the 5 in. pots. Allow only two laterals to grow after the first stopping and remove all other shoots that appear in the leaf axils. As the plant develops it will give the appearance of a letter Y.

The plants should be potted on into final 8 in. pots about the end of May to early June.

Large-flowered Singles should be stopped for the second time around the 14th June and the medium-sized types about the 21st June. After removing the tip of each of the two first breaks (the arms of the letter Y), three breaks should be allowed to grow on each, making six blooms per plant when the Second Crown buds are secured.

Feeding of Singles can usually commence in mid-July, and the general directions about feeding should be followed.

Second Crown buds will begin to appear at the end of the six lateral growths about the end of August, and these should be secured as soon as they can be safely handled without damage to the stems. All the unwanted growths which develop in the leaf axils below the buds should be removed.

Spray Chrysanthemums

Until recently little interest was shown by amateur growers in the Late-flowering Sprays, but the present day trend of floral arrangements has increased the commercial demand for this type of chrysanthemum. Through pressure from their wives, amateurs are being persuaded to grow a few pots of these attractive flowers, in addition to the disbudded cultivars.

Many of the Spray chrysanthemums have been introduced from America and they are often referred to as 'American Sprays'. Their natural flowering time is from early October until early January.

Cuttings should not be rooted until mid-May to obtain plants ready for potting on into final 8 in. pots during July. By using the 'late struck cutting' technique the plants will be approximately 4 ft in height at flowering time. If rooted earlier in the season the plants would reach a height of 8–9 ft at flowering time—most unmanageable for the amateurs greenhouse. To obtain cutting material for mid-May, cuttings from the previous season's plants should be rooted during February and when well rooted transferred into boxes about 4 in. deep. Once the plants are growing away, they should be stopped by removing the growing points. Lateral growths will then develop from the leaf axils and these will provide the cuttings for rooting in May. When rooted, pot on into 3 in. pots during early June; the plants will then be ready for the final potting during July.

After they are in the final pots, their cultural routine is the same as described for other types of Late-flowering chrysanthemums.

6. DECORATIVE POT PLANTS

CHRYSANTHEMUMS DWARFED FOR POT PLANTS

Chrysanthemums as small pot plants have now become extremely popular as sold extensively in florists shops throughout the year. This is a specialised type of cultivation practised in the main by commercial growers and not easily adapted to the average conditions available to the amateur.

Quite briefly the procedure is as follows:- Cuttings about 2 in. in length are rooted in seed boxes. As soon as they are rooted they should immediately be transplanted, five cuttings into a 5 in. pot or one into a $3\frac{1}{2}$ in. pot. They are grown on benches in a greenhouse and control is by means of day length and temperature. Day length control is effected by using black polythene over the plants for fixed periods of time, in order to initiate buds while the plants are still quite dwarf. A chemical known as Phosfon is mixed with the potting soil, or B.9 is sprayed over the plants to retard inter-node elongation, thus keeping the plants dwarf. To increase the number of blooms per pot, the plants are stopped to give two or three breaks per plant.

Cutting material is obtainable from specialist chrysanthemum nurseries. It is extremely important that these cuttings are in fresh vegetative condition and all of equal length. As these are supplied only in large quantities, amateurs would have to keep a stock of stools from which to obtain cutting material. In the main it is the November-flowering types which respond to this treatment.

The most satisfactory time of year for this method of cultivation is from mid-March to the end of December and it is not recommended for amateurs to attempt to flower plants earlier in the year when intensity of daylight is at its lowest.

Those who wish to make a full study of this type of culture should obtain *Chrysanthemums the Year Round* by S. A. Searle & B. J. Machin, published by Blandford Press.

CHARM CHRYSANTHEMUMS

The Charm Chrysanthemum may best be used as a decorative subject, and is grown in pots to flower from the end of October onwards for six to eight weeks.

Seed should be sown in gentle heat about the end of January or early in February, the seedlings pricked out into seed boxes, and then potted on in the usual manner. The plants should be placed outside as soon as the weather is suitable and brought under glass again at the end of September or early October. The final potting should be into 8, 9 or 10 in. pots, according to the size of plants required. As growth proceeds the plants commence to throw out secondary shoots from the base until it is eventually a mass of wiry shoots, each of which finally terminates in a group of flower buds. The fern-like foliage is finely cut and of a pleasing shade of green.

Charm Chrysanthemums arose from a sport of a Cascade Chrysanthemum at Messrs. Suttons of Reading. Although usually raised from seed each year, plants should be propagated from cuttings if special colours are desired, as Charm Chrysanthemums do not come true to colour from seed. The cuttings can be taken from the previous season's plants during February.

CASCADE CHRYSANTHEMUMS

The chrysanthemum most suited to 'cascade' training is a vigorous-growing form, making a much branched plant with long wiry stems and small deeply-cut leaves. It carries daisy-like single flowers, in shades of pink, white, bronze, yellow, scarlet, crimson or rich ruby.

This type of chrysanthemum and method of training have been used for many years both in Japan and China.

The general cultivation as regards potting and care during the growing period is the same as for the Decorative types of chrysanthemum grown in pots. Cuttings may be rooted in December and January and potted on in the usual way, the final potting into 10 in. pots being made in May. The compost for this must be J.I. 4, as the plants are gross feeders. Particular care should be taken that the plants are kept growing freely, and free from insect pests such as greenfly and leafminer.

When the pots are full of roots the plants should be fed regularly twice a week with a balanced chrysanthemum fertilizer.

The method of training to produce the 'cascade' shape which has found most favour is to confine the plant to one, or possibly two, leading shoots at an early stage. Pots are then stood upon a shelf or placed in a trough on a wall facing south. They should be about 5–6 ft above the ground. A bamboo cane should be inserted in the ground in front of each plant, and secured to the pot at an angle just off the perpendicular, down which the leading shoot or shoots may then be trained. All laterals should be stopped at about two or three leaves and stopped again as required to make bushy lateral growth. The leader is allowed to grow on, being tied to the bamboo cane as growth proceeds during the growing season. Discontinue the stopping of lateral growths about the middle of September, and flower buds will commence to appear about the end of the month. The plants will then be approximately 4–6 ft in length.

At the first sign of inclement weather in autumn, the stakes should be removed and the pots placed on a shelf or pedestal in the cool greenhouse. Care must be taken not to damage the stems when moving the plants. When in position in the house, it is advisable to fix the end of the longest shoots to some support to prevent the plants being damaged. Flowers may be expected from the end of October to December, the whole plant being one mass of bloom for several weeks.

Should the 'cascade' form not be required these plants may be grown in an upright position, stopping them twice in the early stages to ensure branching. They will develop into well branched bushy plants 3–4 ft high and 2–3 ft in width, having small single daisy-like flowers which continue to bloom for many weeks. Many of the flowers are delicately scented and, in addition to their value for decoration in pots, are most useful as cut flowers making an unusual and attractive table decoration.

Propagation may also be effected by means of seed. This should be sown in gentle heat from the middle to the end of February, and the resultant seedlings potted on and treated exactly the same as described for rooted cuttings. Seed can only be obtained in mixture and when separate colours are desired plants must be propagated from cuttings.

Cascade chrysanthemums were hardly known outside Japan until 1930. They will appeal especially to those who prefer a natural, very graceful type of plant.

7. PESTS AND DISEASES

With all forms of plant life, there are always pests and diseases to deal with. One of the best forms of defence is to produce strong, healthy plants, as such plants not only resist attack but are often able to recover quickly from many forms of damage. The following list of pests and diseases may appear to be quite formidable, but it is possible for an amateur to grow chrysanthemums for many years without encountering any serious problems, providing the appropriate preventative measures have been practised.

PESTS

Aphids

There are many kinds of aphids but the three species which are most likely to be found on chrysanthemums are:

Chrysanthemum aphid, *Macrosiphoniella sanborni* Gill
Mottled arum aphid, *Aulacorthum circumflexum* Buckt.
Peach-potato aphid, *Myzus persicae Sulz.*

Control: In recent years aphids have been much more difficult to control than in the past. This is undoubtedly due to the emergence of strains which have acquired resistance to the chemical substances that have been used. The method of alternating between two or more chemical controls will be helpful. The range of chemical controls is wide and includes B.H.C., Derris, Malathion, Nicotine and Pyrethrum, used strictly in accordance with the manufacturer's instructions.

Caterpillars

These are the larvae of certain species of moth and are responsible for many kinds of damage. Some caterpillars eat the foliage and may do an immense amount of damage in a short time if unchecked.

Control: Handpicking is a useful control though the camouflage of the caterpillar and its habit of hiding during the day make discovery very difficult. D.D.T. is usually effective and may be applied as a dust or spray.

Capsids

Tarnished plant bug (Bishop bug), *Lygus rugulipennis* Popp.

Common green capsid, *Lygocoris pabulinus* L.

These are green in colour, slightly larger than the house fly, with a flattened and shiny body. They are difficult to detect as they move very quickly over the plant.

Capsids feed by puncturing leaves and stems with their long stylets and frequently turn their attention to the flower buds. The results of their attacks are puckered leaves, blind or distorted shoots and malformed flowers. These pests are possibly the most troublesome of all and, though control is difficult, every effort must be made to keep their numbers down.

Control: The best chemical control is by means of D.D.T., B.H.C. or Malathion. The former is the more persistent and may be applied at fortnightly intervals during the time of peak danger which is July and August.

Earwigs

The common earwig, *Forficula auricularia* L.

This very common pest attacks foliage and flower. It thrives in gardens in which there is plenty of cover to hide during the day, so that general cleanliness will help to reduce the numbers.

Control: Hand-picking is effective at night when the earwigs are feeding, but a more satisfactory control is exercised by trapping them in small pots filled with hay or similar material placed upturned on bamboo canes amongst the plants. Another effective method is to inject paraffin or Three-in-One Oil into the open ends of the canes. This means sudden death to any earwig.

Chemical control is by means of D.D.T. or B.H.C. which may be either dusted or sprayed over the plants.

Eelworm

Leaf and bud eelworm, *Aphelenchoides ritzema-bosi* (Schwartz Stein).

This foliar nematode is quite invisible to the naked eye. It travels up the stems of the plant in a film of water and enters the leaves through the minute breathing pores. Within the leaf they devour the tissue and this results in dead patches which show up first of all as brown areas but later turn black. A feature of these blackened areas is that they are usually bounded by the veins within the leaf and are therefore of a characteristic triangular shape.

Control: The strictest hygiene must be practised. All withered foliage, whether infested or not, must be gathered up immediately and burned.

Amateurs who wish to rid valuable stock of eelworm may do so by subjecting the stools to warm-water treatment. This is given as soon as possible after the plants have become dormant. The stems are cut down and the roots thoroughly washed to remove all the old soil. The washings should not be allowed to contaminate any soil or receptacle which is likely to come into contact with chrysanthemums. After all the surplus water has drained away, the stools are immersed for five minutes in water at 115°F (46°C) and then immediately plunged into cold water.

Froghoppers

The species usually found on chrysanthemums is the common frog-hopper, *Philaenus leucophthalmus* L.

Froghoppers are capable of causing damage at two stages in their life cycle. The first attack comes in early summer when they are seen as small larvae enclosed in a mass of froth which they have produced by extracting sap from the plant. Growth is hindered and distortion sometimes takes place. This is the time to control the pest for it is now at the most vulnerable stage.

Control: Malathion, B.H.C. or Derris will give control but it must come into contact with the pest and this means that the froth must either be removed or penetrated.

Leafminer

This very common pest is the Chrysanthemum Leafminer, *Phytomyza atricornis* Meigen.

The mature insect is a small fly which is rarely seen, the damage being caused in the larval stage. The eggs are laid between the upper and lower skins of the leaves and the first sign of attack will be tiny speckles made by punctures in the skin. As the larva develops it feeds on the inner tissues, tunnelling as it goes and creating the typical white vein-trails seen on the leaves.

Control: Leafminer maggots can be clearly seen in their tunnels and a pinch between thumb and finger will kill them.

Chemical control must be commenced early with a view to keeping the fly away from the stools and cuttings. Nicotine or B.H.C. fumigation will give good control under glass and any maggots which do develop may be killed with B.H.C. sprays.

In the open garden, control is by means of B.H.C. or Malathion sprays. Heavily infested leaves should be removed and burned.

Leafhoppers

Glasshouse leafhoppers, *Erythroneura pallidifrons* Edw.

Potato leafhopper, *Cicadella aurata* Liv.

The symptoms are severe mottling of the leaves caused by the removal of sap by sucking. The insects are extremely active and jump or fly off immediately they are disturbed.

Control: As advised for Capsids.

Stoolminer

Chrysanthemum Stoolminer, *Psila nigrocornis* Meigen.

This is a small two-winged fly very similar in appearance to the carrot fly. It appears in two distinct broods. The first flies appear in May and June and lay their eggs in the soil around newly planted chrysanthemums. The larvae hatch out within a fortnight and begin to feed on the roots.

The activities of the grubs lowers vitality and interferes with the flow of sap, with the result that few cuttings are produced.

Control: B.H.C. is probably the best material available at present and control can be exercised at two distinct periods. B.H.C. Dust may be worked into the top layers of soil at planting time, thus blunting the edge of the first attack, and the same treatment applied during August and September to both Early and Late plants.

Thrips

There are many species of thrips which attack a wide variety of garden plants and the one most frequently associated with the chrysanthemum is the Rose thrip, *Thrips fuscipennis* Hal.

They are small winged insects which can be seen only when they rise in large numbers. Both buds and opening blooms can be attacked and the sucking activities of the thrips causes discolouration and shrivelling of the florets.

Control: In the open garden this is by means of sprays using D.D.T., B.H.C. or Malathion, taking care to spray the undersides of the leaves. Open flowers may be sprayed with a non-persistent material such as Nicotine which should be applied at dusk or in dull conditions. Under glass the same insecticides can be used in the form of a smoke.

Whitefly

The Glasshouse whitefly, *Trialeurodes vaporariorum* Westwood.

This species is active throughout the year and attacks a wide variety of plants. The adults and nymphs feed on the under surfaces of the leaves and may be seen with the naked eye.

Control: D.D.T. or B.H.C. and a combined smoke is often the best answer. Two or three fumigations at fourteen day intervals are usually necessary.

DISEASES

Botrytis

This fungus disease is sometimes known as Grey Mould, a term which well describes its appearance. It is active at temperatures above 40°F (4°C) when the atmosphere is charged with moisture.

Control: Infected material must be removed carefully as soon as it is noticed, taking every precaution to prevent any ripe spores from falling on healthy tissue. In the greenhouse, the best control is obtained by giving such heat and ventilation as is necessary to keep the atmosphere dry and moving.

In the open garden a useful chemical aid in preventing flower loss is Captan which may be sprayed on the buds. To avoid visible deposit one should aim at a fine fog of dust.

Leafy Gall

Leafy Gall is caused by the bacteria, *Corynebacterium fasciens*. The symptoms can hardly be missed or mistaken since they consist of a mass of dwarfed shoots at the base of the stem. The mass looks very much like a cauliflower as it protrudes above the soil surface.

Control: Complete destruction is the only possible treatment since no cure is known for this disease.

Damping-off

This is normally a disease of cuttings and young plants which shows in a basal or collar rot resulting in the complete collapse of the plant at or near soil level. The symptoms may be caused by any one of a number of fungus parasites.

Control: Some of the fungus parasites are easily controlled by watering with Cheshunt Compound as the cuttings are inserted.

Foot and Stem Rot

This has been a troublesome disease for a long time, but only recently has an identification been made. The symptoms are very stunted plants with a yellowing of the lower leaves. In some ways the symptoms are not unlike those of Verticillium Wilt.

Control: Fungicides based on Dithane have been used with some success as a weekly drench but the only really satisfactory course is to move the chrysanthemums away from that particular plot.

Petal Blight
Itersonilia perplexans

This disease is very common on many species of plants and attacks both leaves and flowers. When conditions are suitable for its spread, the attack builds up very quickly and often defies every attempt to control it.

The symptoms first appear as small pinkish spots on the outer florets. In a very short time each spot becomes the centre of an area of wetness which ultimately turns brown.

Control: Chemical aids do exist but they should be looked upon as preventatives not cures. The amateur will obtain fair protection by the use of Captan either as a spray or dust.

Powdery Mildew
Oidium chrysanthemi

A fungus disease which shows itself as a white floury coating. It usually begins on the under surfaces of the older leaves at the base of the plant but will spread to the upper surfaces and the stems if unchecked.

Control: In the open garden the disease can be checked by spraying Karathane or a fungicide based on sulphur. Some growers incorporate such a fungicide with an insecticide as a combined spray towards the end of August.

Verticillium Wilt
Caused by two parasitic fungi: *Verticillium albo-atrum*
Verticillium dahliae

These fungi are very common in all garden soils and some cultivars seem to be highly susceptible whilst others are rarely affected. The fungus enters by the roots and begins to grow up the stems of the plant. In good growing seasons the stem usually grows faster than the fungus inside .and no symptoms are seen until the bud forms and vegetative growth comes to an end. The fungus continues to extend and interferes with the flow of sap thus leading to wilting and a serious lowering of flower quality.

Control: Some chemical controls have been recommended and research goes on to discover more, but up to the present time there is no really effective chemical answer. All infected plants should be burned.

Virus Diseases

In this group is included a great variety of troubles which have only recently been diagnosed with certainty. Some of the unidentified abnormalities of plants are caused by viruses but since they can be diagnosed only with the aid of electron microscopes and other scientific instruments, there is little the amateur can do about them.

THE COLOUR ILLUSTRATIONS

1 Grace Riley

2 Goya

3 Standard

4 John Riley
6 Tracy Waller
8 Cherry Tracy Waller

5 Golden Standard
7 Salmon Tracy Waller
9 Broadway

10 Value
11 Eve Gray

12 Barry Wiggins
14 Countrystyle
16 Derby Ram

13 Bronze Tracy Waller
15 Crimson Pretty Polly
17 Ambition

18 Cloth of Gold
20 Gipsy

19 Early Red Cloak
21 Grandstand

22 Greatness
24 Headliner
26 Irene Arnold

23 Hector Morris
25 James Patilla
27 Jean Symons

28 John Shoesmith
30 Karen Rowe

29 Ken Cooper
31 Leprechaun

32 Lona May 33 Mayflower Seventy
34 Margaret Billitt 35 Mayfield
36 Mexico 37 Oakfield Pearl

38 Parasol
40 Pamela Thompson

39 Pink Sprite
41 Peter Pan

42 Salmon Eve Gray   43 Salmon Margaret Billitt

44 Pretty Polly

45 Redhead
47 Shirley Snowflake
49 Sonny Riley

46 Shirley Glorious
48 Shirley Sensation
50 Strand

51 Yellow Camito
53 Bronze Fred Porter

52 Pink Goldington Queen
54 Cecely Starmer

55 Bronze Brietner
57 Edward Charles

56 Ruby Queen
58 Susan Rowe

59 Yvonne Arnaud   60 Devonia
61 Juanita   62 Queensmere
63 Spectrum   64 Velvet Maid

65 Sweet Seventeen
66 Ken Bacon

67 Sunsprite

68 Deep Yellow Stardust
69 Incurving Stardust
70 Stardust

71 Fenny
73 Crimson Broadway

72 Woolley Sunshine
74 Sheer Bliss

75 Honeyglow
76 Patricia Baby Doll

77 Pamela Baby Doll
78 Brenda Talbot

79 Bill Else
81 Crown of Gold
83 Fair Dinkum

80 Bronze Roodee
82 David Shoesmith
84 Frances Margerison

85 Baby Doll
87 John Perrott
89 Jack Curtis

86 Golden Charm
88 Joe Edwards
90 Golden Market

91 Cricket
93 Gladys Sharpe

92 Sampford
94 Betty Wiggins

95 Keystone
97 Ogston Yellow

96 Lyngford
98 New Penny

99 Ensign
100 Oh Boy

101 Primrose Cricket
103 Red Keystone
105 Skipper

102 Smilin' Thro'
104 Primrose Frances Margerison
106 Rosedew

107 Soccer
109 Harry James
111 Impact

108 Yellow Cricket
110 Charles Hall
112 Iris Riley

113 Staybrite
114 Promise

115 Margaret Riley

116 Marilyn Gates

117 Evelyn Bush

118 Nancy Matthews
120 Stephen Rowe

119 Martin Riley
121 Pat Amos

122 Primrose Ermine
124 Susan Mary
126 Yellow Nuggett

123 Ruth Standley
125 Jane Riley
127 Ernest Avison

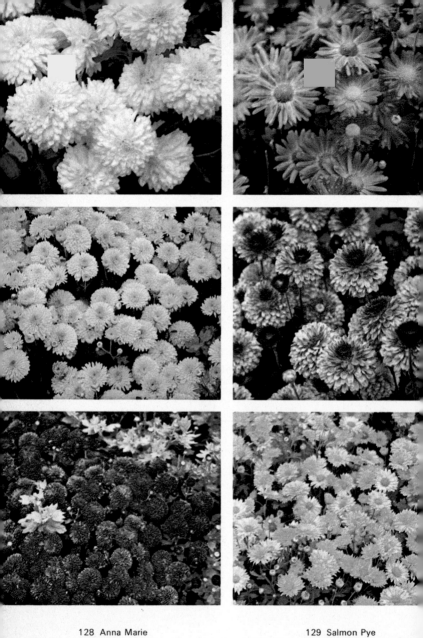

128 Anna Marie
130 Solley
132 Alan

129 Salmon Pye
131 Hunstanton
133 Lemon Tench

134 Pinocchio
136 Poppet
138 Winkie

135 Pamela
137 Fairie
139 Lucida

140 Premiere
141 Aurora

142 Madeleine Queen
143 Adelaine Queen

144 Charming
146 Sweetness

145 Clarette Queen
147 Lilian Hoek

148 Fantastic
150 Pinklea

149 Fairglow
151 Jennifer Squires

152 Carousel
154 Coverack

153 Copeland
155 Glen Rosa

156 Moorland
158 Western Tints

157 Brompton
159 Woolman's Yellow

160 Cheddar

161 Harry Gee

162 James Bryant

169 Rita Jones
171 Shirley Champion

170 Ruby Edwards
172 Jessie Habgood

173 Woking Rose
175 Cream Duke

174 George Edwards
176 Gigantic

177 J. S. Dakers
179 Amethyst

178 Pamela Williams
180 Monica Bennett

181 Shirley Giant
183 Betty Barnes

182 Red Majestic
184 Duke of Kent

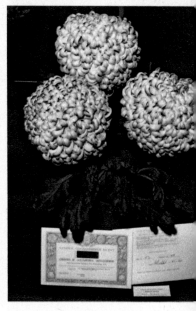

185 Connie Mayhew
187 Golden Wedding

186 Cossack
188 Rita Shirley

189 Audrey Shoesmith

190 Frances Jefferson

191 Dexta

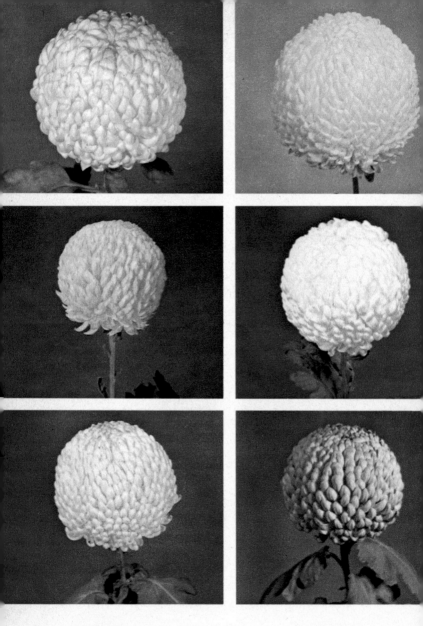

192 Dorridge Cream
194 Langley
196 Mary Ann Royles

193 John Rowe
195 Marjorie Montague
197 Mavis Shoesmith

198 Minstrel Boy

199 Maylen

200 Severn

201 Shirley Imp
202 Shirley Model

203 Waterloo
204 Dorothy Whittock

205 Golden Maylen
206 Red Shirley Model

207 Woolman's Perfecta

208 Edward Rowe

209 Ron Shoesmith

210 Vera Woolman

211 Shirley Empress

212 Brett Williams

213 Goldkist

214 Woolman's Temptation

215 Yellow Ron Shoesmith

216 Flashpoint
218 London Gazette
220 Apricot My Lady

217 Halloween
219 Elizabeth Deeley
221 Polar Gem

222 Primrose Mona Davis
224 Walker's Jewel
226 Deep Pink Joy Hughes

223 Stuart Shoesmith
225 Capri
227 Joy Hughes

228 Yellow Princess Anne

229 Apricot Princess Anne

230 Princess Anne

231 Crimson Lake

232 Copper Globe

233 Bridal Gown

234 My Lady   235 Chantilly

236 Yellow Symbol

237 Elizabeth Woolman
239 Shirley Garnet
241 Kingsway

238 State Fair
240 Avenger
242 James Bond

243 Bronze Mayford Perfection
244 Red Mayford Perfection
245 Primrose Mayford Perfection
246 Yellow Mayford Perfection
247 Mayford Perfection
248 Purple Mayford Perfection
249 Dark Red Mayford Perfection
250 Rose Mayford Perfection

251 Rylands Gold
253 Cary Hodgson
255 Watcombe

252 Doris Squires
254 Gold Foil
256 Rose Shoesmith

257 Robert Shoesmith
259 St. Moritz
261 Yellow Balcombe Perfection

258 Olympic Queen
260 John Marksam
262 Brenda Till

263–271 Mavis Shoesmith, Polar Gem, Minstrel Boy, Woking Perfection, Dorridge Cream, Yellow Maylen, Red Shirley Model, Shirley Model, Penguin

272–274 Balcombe Perfection, Amber Balcombe Perfection. Red Balcombe Perfection

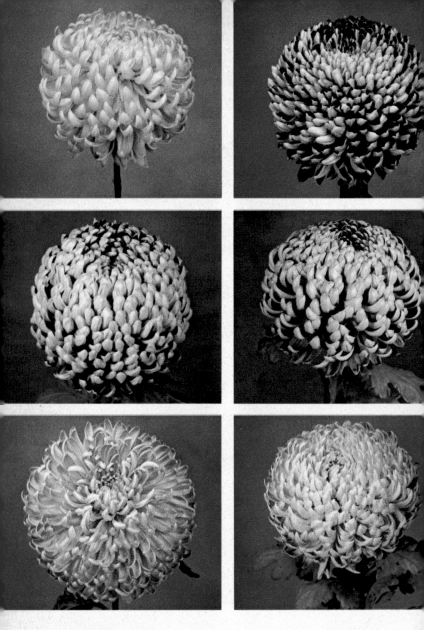

275 Orange Fair Lady
277 Lagoon
279 Bronze Fair Lady

276 Leslie Tandy
278 Sheridan
280 Elizabeth Burton

281 Group of Charms and Cascades
282 Mary Selvey

283 Mary Jefferies
285 Gold Digger
287 Thora

284 Fair Lady
286 Beacon
288 Uranus

289 Daily Mirror
291 Harmony
293 Edwin Painter

290 Copper Choice
292 Elsie May
294 Sunsilk

295 Pink Cascade
296 White Cascade
297 Chesswood Beauty
298 Marigold

299 Yellow Charm
300 Red Charm

301 Woolman's Glory
302 Sun Valley

303 Albert Cooper
305 Annina
307 Cleone

304 Midlander
306 Broadacre
308 Golden Woolman's Glory

309 Nancy Sherwood
311 Jinx
313 Red Woolman's Glory

310 Preference
312 Peggy Stevens
314 Yellow Cleone

315 Fred Sherwood
317 Alliance

316 Alice Fitton
318 Rona (Single)

319 Tokio

320 Anemone Collection

321–325 Long Island Beauty, Galaxy,
Red Rolinda, Yellow Galaxy, Iceberg

326 Rayonnante Collection

327 Tuneful

328 Spidery Collection

329 Shasta
331 Red Galaxy
333 Tafetta

330 Minstrel
332 Yellow Galaxy
334 Yellow Tafetta

335 Sylphide
337 Ross Cleone
340 Green Nightingale

336 Harriet Sherwood
338 and 339 Flying Saucer, Raymond Mounsey
341 Jane Key

342 Apricot Shoesmith Salmon   343 Yellow Shoesmith Salmon
344 Shoesmith Salmon   345 Cerise Shoesmith Salmon
346 Ruby Shoesmith Salmon   347 Golden Rival's Rival
348 Bronze Shoesmith Salmon   349 Rival's Rival

8.   CLASSIFICATION OF CHRYSANTHEMUMS

The National Chrysanthemum Society of Great Britain has a classification into which the many thousands of chrysanthemums now in cultivation may be grouped according to the shape or formation of the bloom.

The six main groups are as follows:

1 INCURVED
   Cultivars in this group have blooms with close, firm, tightly incurved florets forming a perfect globe.
2 REFLEXED
   This group includes cultivars that have dropping florets which should reflex gracefully and overlap one another to give a fully-reflexed bloom. Those types with quilled, sharply-pointed florets which stand out stiffly are also included in this group.
3 INTERMEDIATE
   This group includes blooms which are not completely incurved or true reflexed types. Cultivars in this group have blooms with florets which incurve closely and regularly or loosely and irregularly, but do not form a perfect globe. Other types included in this group are those with semi-reflexing florets.
4 ANEMONE
   This group consists of single cultivars that have tubular disk florets forming a central cushion.
5 POMPON
   This group is composed of very small-flowered cultivars.
6 SINGLES
   This group includes all cultivars (other than Anemones) which have approximately five rows of ray florets and a visible central disk (or 'daisy-eye').

There is a further division of cultivars according to the normal time of flowering. The divisions are numbered from Section 1 to Section 30 as follows:

LATE-FLOWERING CHRYSANTHEMUMS
(USUALLY FLOWERED UNDER GLASS)

Section 1. Large Exhibition
Reflexing and Incurving

Section 2. Medium Exhibition

Section 3. Exhibition Incurved
(a) Large-flowered
(b) Medium-flowered

Section 4. Reflexed Decoratives
(a) Large-flowered
(b) Medium-flowered

Two main types may be distinguished:

A. The fully reflexing type has florets which reflex gracefully; they may interlace and/or whorl according to the recognised form of the cultivar. They may reflex vertically from the 'shoulder' or inwards towards the stem.

B. The type with stiff florets which do not form a 'shoulder'. The outline, though spiky, is symmetrical with breadth and depth in proportion.

Section 5. Intermediate Decoratives
(a) Large-flowered
(b) Medium-flowered

Three main types of bloom are distinguished:

A. Blooms with florets incurving to give a generally globular outline but with an open floret formation showing the inner colour. This type rarely closes at the centre.

B. Blooms with florets incurving to give a generally globular outline with a closer floret formation showing very little of the inner colour. This type may sometimes close at the centre.

C. Blooms formed of lower florets reflexing to reveal the inner colour but with the upper florets incurving to show the reverse colour.

Section 6. Anemones
(a) Large-flowered
(b) Medium-flowered

Section 7. Singles
      (a) Large-flowered
      (b) Medium-flowered

Section 8. Pompons

Section 9. Sprays
      (a) Anemones
      (b) Pompons
      (c) Reflexing
      (d) Singles

Section 10. Spidery, etc.

Section 11. Any Other Types

OCTOBER-FLOWERING CHRYSANTHEMUMS

Section 13. Incurved Decoratives
      (a) Large-flowered
      (b) Medium-flowered

Section 14. Reflexed Decoratives
      (a) Large-flowered
      (b) Medium-flowered
      Two main types may be distinguished:
      A. The fully reflexing type has florets which reflex gracefully; they may interlace and/or whorl according to the recognised form of the cultivar. They may reflex vertically from the 'shoulder' or inwards towards the stem.
      B. The type with stiff florets which do not form a 'shoulder'. The outline, though spiky, is symmetrical with breadth and depth in proportion.

Section 15. Intermediate Decoratives
      (a) Large-flowered
      (b) Medium-flowered
      Three main types of bloom are distinguishable:
      A. Blooms with florets incurving to give a generally globular outline but with an open floret formation showing the inner colour. This type rarely closes at the centre.

B. Blooms with florets incurving to give a generally globular outline with a closer floret formation showing very little of the inner colour. This type may sometimes close at the centre.

C. Blooms formed of lower florets reflexing to reveal the inner colour but with the upper florets incurving to show the reverse colour.

Section 16. Large October-flowering

Section 17. Singles
    (a) Large-flowered
    (b) Medium-flowered

Section 18. Pompons

Section 19. Sprays
    (a) Anemones
    (b) Pompons
    (c) Reflexing
    (d) Singles

Section 20. Any Other Types

Sections 21/22. These have been reserved for any new types which may be introduced in the future.

EARLY-FLOWERING CHRYSANTHEMUMS

An Early-flowering Chrysanthemum is a cultivar which blooms in a normal season in the open ground before 1st October without any protection whatsoever.

Section 23. Incurved Decoratives
    (a) Large-flowered
    (b) Medium-flowered

Section 24. Reflexed Decoratives
    (a) Large-flowered
    (b) Medium-flowered
    Two main types may be distinguished:
    A. The fully reflexing type has florets which reflex gracefully;

they may interlace and/or whorl according to the recognised form of the cultivar. They may reflex vertically from the 'shoulder' or inward towards the stem.

B. The type with stiff florets which do not form a 'shoulder'. The outline, though spiky, is symmetrical with breadth and depth in proportion.

Section 25. Intermediate Decoratives

    (a) Large-flowered

    (b) Medium-flowered

Three main types of bloom are distinguishable:

A. Blooms with florets incurving to give a generally globular outline but with an open floret formation showing the inner colour. This type rarely closes at the centre.

B. Blooms with florets incurving to give a generally globular outline with a closer floret formation showing very little of the inner colour. This type may sometimes close at the centre.

C. Blooms formed of lower florets reflexing to reveal the inner colour but with the upper florets incurving to show the reverse colour.

Section 26. Anemones

Section 27. Singles

    (a) Large-flowered

    (b) Medium-flowered

Section 28. Pompons

    (a) True Poms

    (b) Semi-Poms

Section 29. Sprays

    (a) Anemones

    (b) Pompons

    (c) Reflexing

    (d) Singles

Section 30. Any Other Types

Note: In the N.C.S. Classification all cultivars are classified according to the flower type so that Koreans are dealt with as either Singles, Pompons or Sprays.

COLOUR CLASSIFICATION

The colour classification does not give the precise colour of a cultivar. It is merely a general classification to assist exhibitors and judges to decide whether a particular cultivar is or is not eligible to be shown in a particular class. For example, cultivars that are cream in colour are classified as pale yellow; orange cultivars are classified as yellow; and crimson cultivars are classified as red.

KEY TO COLOUR CLASSIFICATION

B	Bronze	S	Salmon
LB	Light Bronze	W	White
P	Pink	Y	Yellow
PP	Pale Pink	PY	Pale Yellow
Pu	Purple	O	Other Colours.
R	Red		

9. DESCRIPTIONS OF CULTIVARS

The descriptions which follow are listed in the same numbered sequence as the coloured illustrations. The Plate Number is followed by the name of the cultivar, the National Chrysanthemum Society's classification, the colour classification, the name of the Raiser, the year of introduction and the Award, if any, granted to the cultivar by the National Chrysanthemum Society. Finally, a general description to assist identification.

In respect of the habit and vigour of the plant and the flowering season, the time of flowering and the height of the plant must be considered as approximate. Variations will occur due to the environmental conditions under which the plants are grown together with the geographical location.

Where groups of chrysanthemums are illustrated together, the reader will be able to identify each bloom from the description.

Chrysanthemums in the main when grown under natural conditions have a flowering period in Great Britain from mid-August to the end of December. They are grown successfully in other countries where the climatic conditions are similar.

(i) EARLY-FLOWERING CHRYSANTHEMUMS

1 **Grace Riley.** 24a B. RILEY 1970. Award of Merit.
Reflexed form. Florets are copper bronze shading to light bronze at the tips, gracefully building up to make a bloom of good depth. Height approx. 4 ft – September.

2 **Goya.** 24a LB. RILEY 1964. Award of Merit.
Reflexed form. Light bronze florets which interlace and/or whorl. Height approx. 3 ft – September.

3 **Standard.** 24a B. SHOESMITH 1959.
Reflexed form. Copper bronze florets of good substance which gracefully build up to give a classical bloom of good breadth and depth. One of the best large bronze reflexed types. Height approx. 4 ft – September.

4 **John Riley.** 24a R. RILEY 1970. Award of Merit.
Reflexed form. Deep crimson florets with a velvet sheen. Good foliage. Height approx. 3 ft 6 in. – September.

5 **Golden Standard.** 24a Y. PARR 1967.
Yellow sport from Standard.
Reflexed form. Has all the good characteristics of the parent. Height approx. 4 ft – September.

6 **Tracy Waller.** 24a P. RILEY 1963. Award of Merit.
Reflexed form. Deep pink florets tinged salmon/blue, with interlace and/or whorl. Height approx. 4 ft – September.

7 **Salmon Tracy Waller.** 24a S. RILEY 1965. Sport from Tracy Waller.
Salmon pink florets with the same characteristics as the parent. Height approx. 4 ft – September.

8 **Cherry Tracy Waller.** 24a R. RILEY 1966. Sport from Tracy Waller.
Red Bronze florets with the same characteristics as the parent. Height approx. 4 ft – September.

9 **Broadway.** 24b Pu. RILEY 1964.
Classical reflexed form. Deep purple florets of good substance. Dark green foliage. Height approx. 4 ft 6 in. – September.

10 **Value.** 24b LB. RILEY 1964.
Classical reflexed form. Light bronze florets tinged with a deeper shade of bronze. Solid bloom and good foliage. Height approx. 3 ft 6 in. – September.

11 **Eve Gray.** 24b PP. RILEY 1966. Award of Merit.
Classical reflexed form. Pale pink florets with salmon-blue tinge. Height approx. 4 ft – September.

12 **Barry Wiggins.** 24b LB. WIGGINS 1961.
Reflexed form. Light golden bronze florets. Very neat and compact bloom. Height approx. 3 ft 6 in. – September.

13 **Bronze Tracy Waller.** 24a B. RILEY 1966. Bronze sport of Tracy Waller.
Reflexed form. Mid-bronze florets which interlace and/or whorl. Height approx. 4 ft – September.

14 **Countrystyle.** 24b LB. RILEY 1967. Preliminary Commendation.
Reflexed form. Warm apricot-bronze florets tinged with green towards the centre. Good cut flower type. Height approx. 4 ft – September.

15 **Crimson Pretty Polly.** 24b R. RILEY 1966. Crimson sport from Pretty Polly.
Classical reflexed form. Rich crimson

florets with velvet sheen. Dwarf and vigorous in growth. Height approx. 3 ft 3 in. – September.

16 Derby Ram. 24a B. RILEY 1968. Preliminary Commendation.
Reflexed form. Florets a warm bronze colour. Good solid bloom of classical form. Height approx. 4 ft – September.

17 Ambition. 24a Y. JOHNSON 1969. Preliminary Commendation.
Reflexed form. Deep yellow broad florets. Natural and perfect reflexed formation to give a good depth. Height approx. 3 ft 6 in. – September.

18 Cloth of Gold. 24b Y. WOOLMAN 1969. Preliminary Commendation.
Reflexed form. Light straw coloured. Good cut flower type. Height 3 ft 6 in. – September.

19 Early Red Cloak. 24b R. SHOESMITH 1964.
Reflexed form. Deep red rolled florets. Good solid bloom. Dark green foliage. Very reliable. Height approx. 3 ft 9 in. – September.

20 Gipsy. 24b R. RILEY 1960. Award of Merit.
Reflexed form. Rich crimson florets with velvet sheen. Classical type, good depth. Dark green foliage. Height approx. 3 ft 6 in. – September.

21 Grandstand. 24a B. RILEY 1966.
Reflexed form. Rich copper/bronze florets of good substance. Very large blooms with slight tendency to coarseness. Useful type for the exhibitor. Height approx. 4 ft – September.

22 Greatness. 24a Y. RILEY 1964.
Reflexed form. Clear yellow florets which build up to give a very solid bloom. Useful type for the exhibitor.

Strong grower. Height approx. 4 ft – September.

23 Hector Morris. 24b B. RILEY 1961. Award of Merit.
Reflexed form. Mid-bronze florets. Plants will carry a good crop of weatherproof blooms suitable for garden display or exhibition. Height approx. 4 ft – September.

24 Headliner. 24a P. ROWE 1961. Award of Merit.
Reflexed form. Deep pink florets tinged with blue which interlace and/or whorl. Height approx. 4 ft – September.

25 James Patilla. 24a Y. PATILLA/JOHNSON 1962. Award of Merit.
Classical reflexed form. Florets deep clear yellow which build up to give a very solid bloom. Tendency to softness if undercropped and grown too large. Height approx. 3 ft 6 in. – September.

26 Irene Arnold. 24b P. ROWE 1970. Award of Merit.
Classical reflexed form. Pale pink florets with salmon tinge. Good foliage. Height approx. 3 ft 6 in. – September.

27 Jean Symons. 24b P. WILSON 1967. Award of Merit.
Deep reflexed form. Florets deep pink with a blue tinge. Height approx. 3 ft 6 in. – September.

28 John Shoesmith. 24a R. SHOESMITH 1961.
Classical reflexed form. Deep crimson florets of good substance. Vigorous grower. Height approx. 3 ft 6 in. – September.

29 Ken Cooper. 24a Y. RILEY 1964. Award of Merit.
Reflexed form. Clear yellow florets of good substance. Suitable for garden dis-

play or exhibition. Height approx. 3 ft 6 in. – September.

30 **Karen Rowe.** 24a P. ROWE 1969.
Reflexed form. Florets salmon/pink shade. An attractive garden flower. height approx. 3 ft 6 in. – September.

31 **Leprechaun.** 24b P. RILEY 1969. Preliminary Commendation.
Classical reflexed form. Florets purplish pink. Good garden type. Height approx. 5 ft – September.

32 **Lona May.** 24a Y. SHOESMITH/HEDLEY COOK 1967. Award of Merit.
Reflexed form. Clear mid-yellow florets. Vigorous grower. Height approx. 4 ft – September.

33 **Mayflower Seventy.** 24a R. WOOLMAN 1969. Preliminary Commendation.
Reflexed form. Reddish bronze florets. Nice foliage. Height approx. 4 ft 6 in. – September.

34 **Margaret Billitt.** 24a Pu. RILEY 1964. Award of Merit.
Reflexed form. Cyclamen purple florets which build up to give a bloom of great depth. An exhibitor's flower. Height approx. 4 ft – September.

35 **Mayfield.** 24b Y. PATILLA/JOHNSON 1966.
Classical reflexed form. Pale yellow florets develop• to give a bloom with good shoulders. Strong grower. Dark green foliage. Height approx. 3 ft 6 in. – September.

36 **Mexico.** 24a R. RILEY 1968. Award of Merit for Exhibition.
Reflexed form. Florets deep cherry red which interlace and/or whorl. Good dark green foliage. A very reliable cultivar. Height approx. 3 ft 6 in. – September.

37 **Oakfield Pearl.** 24b S. H. WALKER 1967.
Reflexed form. Florets pale salmon shading to off-white – this pastel shade is most attractive, particularly for cut flower purposes. Height approx. 3 ft – September.

38 **Parasol.** 24a P. RILEY 1966. Award of Merit.
Classical reflexed form. Orchid pink florets. Good foliage. An exhibitor's flower. Height approx. 3 ft 6 in. – September.

39 **Pink Sprite.** 24b P. RILEY 1969. Preliminary Commendation.
Reflexed form. Florets an attractive shell pink shade. Height approx. 3 ft 6 in. – September.

40 **Pamela Thompson.** 24b W. J. EDWARDS 1965. Preliminary Commendation.
Classical reflexed form. Narrow rolled white florets that give a bloom of good depth – suitable for the exhibitor. Height approx. 3 ft 6 in. – September.

41 **Peter Pan.** 24b B. RILEY 1960.
Reflexed form. Copper bronze florets of good substance. Very reliable and weatherproof. Height approx. 4 ft – September.

42 **Salmon Eve Gray.** 24b S. RILEY 1970.
Reflexed sport from Eve Gray, the difference being that the florets are salmon-pink in colour, otherwise the plant has all the characteristics of the parent.

43 **Salmon Margaret Billitt.** 14a S. WALKER 1968. Sport from Margaret Billitt.
Reflexed form. Florets of deep red salmon colour that interlace and/or

whorl like the parent. Suitable only for show purposes.

44 Pretty Polly. 24b Pu. RILEY 1963.
Neatly reflexing florets of rich purple highlighted by the silver-grey centre. Very weatherproof. Height approx. 3 ft – September.

45 Redhead. 24b R. RILEY 1969. Preliminary Commendation.
Reflexed form. Bronze-red florets of good substance. Height approx. 3 ft 6 in. – September.

46 Shirley Glorious. 24a R. WOOLMAN 1967. Preliminary Commendation.
Reflexed form. Most impressive crimson-red florets. An attractive garden flower, although a little short of petal in the centre. Height approx. 4 ft – September.

47 Shirley Snowflake. 24b W. WOOLMAN 1969. Preliminary Commendation.
Classical reflexed form. Broad florets of glistening white. Height approx. 4 ft – September.

48 Shirley Sensation. 24a B. WOOLMAN 1969. Preliminary Commendation.
Reflexed form. Amber bronze florets that build up to make a large solid bloom. Height approx. 4 ft – September.

49 Sonny Riley. 24b Y. RILEY 1960. Award of Merit.
Classical reflexed form. Clear mid-yellow florets that overlap gracefully to give a refined bloom. (Stock must be selected.) Height 3 ft 6 in. – September.

50 Strand. 24a P. RILEY 1963.
Reflexed form. Crisp long rose-pink florets that interlace and/or whorl. A flower for the showman. Height 3 ft 6 in. – September.

51 Yellow Camito. 24a Y. BURGESS/WILSON 1965. Preliminary Commendation. Sport from Camito.
Classical reflexed form. Florets crisp clear yellow. Has all the characteristics of its white-coloured parent. Height 4 ft 6 in. – September.

52 Pink Goldington Queen. 25a PP. BUCKHAVEN 1966. Sport from Goldington Queen.
Grouped in the Intermediate section because of the variation in form due to geographical and cultural conditions. At its best, a perfect shell-pink reflexed bloom, for the showman. Height 4 ft 6 in. – September.

53 Bronze Fred Porter 24b B. PATILLA/JOHNSON 1967. Sport from Fred Porter.
Reflexed form. Rich bronze florets, hard and weatherproof, enhanced by very light foliage. Height approx. 4 ft 6 in. – September.

54 Cecely Starmer. 24a P. RILEY 1967. Award of Merit.
Reflexed form. Rose-pink florets that remain colourfast. Vigorous habit. Ideal type for exhibition. Height 3 ft 6 in. – September.

55 Bronze Brietner. 24b LB. HOLLAND/WALKER 1965. Sport from Brietner.
Reflexed form. Florets warm apricot shade. Blooms carried on upright stems. Ideal for garden display and cut flowers. Height approx. 4 ft – September.

56 Ruby Queen. 24b R. WOOLMAN 1969.
Reflexed form. Blooms very pretty with their spiky florets. Good centres and attractive foliage. Height 4 ft – September.

57 Edward Charles. 24b W. GURR/WILSON 1970.
Reflexed form. Hard white florets. Full

centres. Dwarf habit and small foliage. Height approx. 3 ft 6 in. – September.

58 Susan Rowe. 24b P. ROWE 1966. Award of Merit.
Reflexed form. Bright rose-pink florets. Blooms carried on good stems. Ideal garden type flower. Height approx 4 ft – September.

59 Yvonne Arnaud. 24a Pu. SHOESMITH/JEFFERIES 1967. Preliminary Commendation.
Reflexed form. Florets of a warm purple shade. Blooms carried on stiff upright stems. Weatherproof. Excellent garden and cut flower type. Height approx. 4 ft – September.

60 Devonia. 24b PY. PATILLA/JOHNSON 1966.
Reflexed form. Florets deep shade of cream that fall to make a classical reflexed bloom for the exhibitor. Height approx. 3 ft – September.

61 Juanita. 24b PY. WOOLMAN 1967.
Reflexed form. Florets warm apricot on the shoulder, changing to a creamy primrose at the petal edge. Height approx. 3 ft 6 in. – September.

62 Queensmere. 24b B. RILEY 1965.
Reflexed form. Florets bright medium-bronze. This is a cut flower or show chrysanthemum. Height approx. 3 ft 6 in. – September.

63 Spectrum. 24a Y. RILEY 1957.
Reflexed form. Clear yellow florets that overlap gracefully to give a compact bloom. Height 4 ft – September.

64 Velvet Maid. 24b R. SHOESMITH/JEFFERIES 1967. Award of Merit.
Reflexed form. Rich crimson florets with velvet sheen. Height approx. 3 ft 6 in. – September.

65 Sweet Seventeen. 20 P. WOOLMAN 1963. Award of Merit.
Grouped in Section 20 – Any Other Types. A chrysanthemum of unusual form – similar to a cactus-type Dahlia, with pale pink spiky florets. An attractive garden and cut flower type. Height approx. 4 ft – September.

66 Ken Bacon. 24a P. JOHNSON 1970.
Classical reflexed form. Florets light pink with a blue tinge. Good foliage. Height approx. 3 ft – September.

67 Sunsprite. 25a B. BELL 1964.
Reflexed form. Crisp rolled florets of orange bronze shade. Medium-sized foliage. Height approx. 4 ft – September.

68 Deep Yellow Stardust. 24b Y. BELL 1966. Preliminary Commendation.
Stiff florets that give a spiky outline. Deep yellow sport from Stardust. Height approx. 3 ft 6 in. – August-September.

69 Incurving Stardust. BELL 1964.
Incurving form of Stardust. Height approx. 3 ft 6 in. – September.

70 Stardust. 24b Y. BELL 1958.
Canary yellow crisp rolled florets growing in perfect star-shaped form. Weatherproof and reliable. Height approx. 3 ft 6 in. – August-September.

71 Fenny. 24b PP. ROWE 1968. Trial Ground Award.
Reflexed form. Florets of shell pink – a very attractive pastel shade. Height approx. 4 ft 6 in. – September.

72 Woolley Sunshine. 24b Y. RILEY 1970.
Classical reflexed form. Florets clear mid-yellow that overlap gracefully to make a neat compact bloom. Height approx. 4 ft – September.

73 Crimson Broadway. 24b R. RILEY 1970. Sport from Broadway.
Classical reflexed form. Florets rich dark crimson with velvet sheen. Dark green foliage providing an excellent foil to the bloom. Height approx. 4 ft 6 in. – September.

74 Sheer Bliss. 24a P. RILEY 1970. Award of Merit.
Reflexed form. Soft blue-pink florets that interlace and/or whorl to make a most attractive flower. Height approx. 4 ft – September.

75 Honeyglow. 24a LB. SHOESMITH 1964. Award of Merit.
Reflexed form. Florets rich orange-bronze. The full flowers are borne on long stems. Compact plant. Height approx. 4 ft – September.

76 Patricia Baby Doll. 25b LB. F. C. MILES 1967.
Incurving form. Copper-bronze florets. Very compact and prolific ideal garden plant. Height approx. 4 ft – September.

77 Pamela Baby Doll. 25b S. F. C. MILES 1966. Sport from Baby Doll.
Incurving form. Salmon pink florets. Very compact and prolific, ideal garden plant. Height approx. 4 ft – September.

78 Brenda Talbot. 25b P. SHOESMITH 1953. Award of Merit.
Incurving form. Carnation pink florets of good texture. Upright stems. Dark green foliage. Height approx. 4 ft 6 in. – September.

79 Bill Else. 25b Y. RILEY 1966. Award of Merit.
Incurving form. Florets bright yellow, hard waxy texture. Height 4 ft – September.

80 Bronze Roodee. 25b B. H. WALKER 1967. Preliminary Commendation.
Incurving form. Inner florets rich bronze with golden reverse. Resistant to weather damage. Height approx. 4 ft 6 in. – September.

81 Crown of Gold. 25a Y. SHOESMITH 1963.
Incurving form Rich golden yellow florets, very full in the centre. Dark green foliage. An exhibitor's flower. Height approx. 4 ft – September.

82 David Shoesmith/23a B. SHOESMITH/ JEFFERIES 1970. Preliminary Commendation.
Tight globular incurved form. Inside of florets red with bronze reverse. Good solid bloom. Height approx. 4 ft 6 in. – September.

83 Fair Dinkum. 25b Y. RILEY 1961. Award of Merit.
Incurving form. Florets rich chrome yellow, hard waxy texture. Weather resistant and reliable. Dark green foliage. Height approx. 5 ft – September.

84 Frances Margerison. 25a W. RILEY 1965. Award of Merit.
Incurving form. Broad waxy florets of pure white. A flower for the exhibitor. Height approx. 4 ft – September.

85 Baby Doll. 23b PP. RILEY 1960.
Tight incurved form. Pale pink florets of hard texture. Very prolific weatherproof and reliable garden flower. Height approx. 4 ft – September.

86 Golden Charm. 25b LB. RILEY 1967. Award of Merit.
Loose incurving form. Broad golden bronze florets. A good garden type and useful for the exhibitor. Height approx. 3 ft 6 in. – September.

87 John Perrott. 25a Y. RILEY 1970. Award of Merit.

Incurving form. Broad bright yellow hard florets. The bloom is full in the centre and finishes well. Useful type for the exhibitor. Height approx. 4 ft – September.

88 Joe Edwards. 25a W. RILEY 1963.

Tight incurving form. Pure white broad florets that develop into a well finished bloom for the exhibitor. Height approx. 4 ft – September.

89 Jack Curtis. 25a Y. WIGGINS 1963. Award of Merit.

Loose incurving form. Large broad florets of bright mimosa yellow. Very full centres. Ideal for the showman. Height approx 4 ft – September.

90 Golden Market. 25b LB. ROWE 1970. Preliminary Commendation.

Incurving form. Good hard florets of rich golden bronze colour. Suitable for cut flower or show work. Height approx. 4 ft – September.

91 Cricket. 25b W. RILEY 1961. Award of Merit.

Tight incurving form. Hard white florets of excellent texture. Neat compact growth. Good all purpose chysanthemum. Height approx. 3 ft 6 in. – September.

92 Sampford. 14a LB. ROWE 1964.

Bright orange-flame florets that overlap gracefully to give a neat compact bloom. Upright habit and carries a good crop of flowers. Height approx. 4 ft – September and October.

93 Gladys Sharpe. 25a Y. RILEY 1960.

Incurving form. Broad rich yellow florets of immense size and good quality. The plant is vigorous and easy to grow. Excellent for garden and ex-hibition purposes. Height approx. 3 ft 6 in. – September.

94 Betty Wiggins. 25a Y. WIGGINS 1962.

A butter yellow incurved with good pro-portions. Broad petals which incurve naturally. The foliage is light green, clean and healthy. The plant is dwarf in growth and easy to grow. Height 3 ft – September.

95 Keystone. 25a Pu. RILEY 1963. Award of Merit.

Loosely incurving form. Broad florets royal purple on the inside with a subtle silver reverse. A good chrysanthemum for the exhibitor or cut flower purposes. Height approx. 4 ft – September.

96 Lyngford. 25b P. ROWE 1968.

Incurving form. Broad rich rosy purple florets with silver reverse. Upright grower. Good foliage. Height approx. 3 ft 3 in. – September.

97 Ogston Yellow. 25b Y. RILEY 1969. Preliminary Commendation.

Incurving form. Rich yellow hard florets of good form. Dark green foliage and compact habit. Height approx. 4 ft – September.

98 New Penny. 25a B. RILEY 1970. Pre-liminary Commendation.

Incurving form. Rich bronze inner florets with light bronze reverse. Height approx. 4 ft – September.

99 Ensign. 25b W. ROWE 1969. Pre-liminary Commendation.

Tight incurving form. White florets shading to pink at the bottom. Very hard and weatherproof. Excellent garden flower. Height approx. 3 ft 6 in. – September.

100 Oh Boy. 25b W. RILEY 1960.

Loosely incurving form. Broad white

florets of superb form. Strong grower. Good habit. Height approx. 4 ft – September.

101 Primrose Cricket. 25b PY. THISTLE-THWAITE 1963 Sport from Cricket.
Tight incurving form. Hard pale yellow florets of excellent texture. Neat compact growth. Has all the good characteristics of the parent. Height approx. 3 ft 6 in. – September.

102 Smilin' Thro' 25a P. RILEY 1968.
Loosely incurving form. Purple pink florets with silver reverse, making an attractive bi-coloured chrysanthemum. Height approx. 3 ft 6 in. – September.

103 Red Keystone. 25a R. OLDHAM 1966. Sport from Keystone.
Loosely incurving form. Inner florets red-bronze with copper bronze reverse. Good chrysanthemum for the exhibitor or for cut flower purposes. Height approx. 4 ft – September.

104 Primrose Frances Margerison. 25a PY. RILEY 1970. Preliminary Commendation.
Incurving form. Pale yellow florets of good texture. A flower for the exhibitor. Height approx. 4 ft – September.

105 Skipper. 23b LB. RILEY 1966.
Tightly incurving to give a globular form. Light bronze florets of a hard texture, highly resistant to damping. Height approx. 3 ft – September.

106 Rosedew. 25a P. WOOLMAN 1962.
Loosely incurving form. Broad pink florets with a bluish tinge. Hard texture. Weather resistant. A good all-round chrysanthemum for cut flower and exhibition work. Height approx. 3 ft – September.

107 Soccer. 25a Y. RILEY 1970. Award of Merit.
Loosely incurving form. Very large broad rich butter yellow florets. Full centres. Rather a long neck, although a useful type for the exhibitor. Height approx. 4 ft – September.

108 Yellow Cricket. 25b Y. RILEY/THISTLETHWAITE 1964. Sport from Cricket.
Tight incurving form. Hard yellow florets of excellent texture. Neat compact growth. Has all the good characteristics of the parent. Height approx. 3 ft 6 in. – September.

109 Harry James. 25a B. SHOESMITH 1959.
Loosely incurving form. Rich bronze inner florets with copper bronze reverse. Good centre. Excellent for show work. Height approx. 3 ft 6 in. – September.

110 Charles Hall. 23a O. HALL 1968.
Tightly incurved form. The inner side of the florets of rich crimson with a slight trace of bronze on the reverse. Large blooms of unique colour and texture. Height approx. 3 ft 6 in. – September.

111 Impact. 23b Y. RILEY 1969. Preliminary Commendation.
Tightly incurved form. Broad butter yellow florets of very hard texture. Ideal for garden or exhibition. The dark green foliage provides a perfect foil for the flowers. Height approx. 3 ft 6 in. – September.

112 Iris Riley. 23b P. RILEY 1964. Award of Merit.
Tight incurved form to give a globular bloom. Broad purplish pink florets with waxy sheen. Height approx. 4 ft – September.

113 **Staybrite.** 25b Y. RILEY 1968.
Tightly incurved form. Broad butter yellow florets of hard texture. Full centres. Neat foliage. A good all-purpose chrysanthemum for garden and exhibition. Height approx. 3 ft 6 in. – September.

114 **Promise.** 25a PP. RILEY 1963.
Incurving form that builds up to a ball-shaped bloom. Florets rose-pink with silver reverse. Height approx. 3 ft – September.

115 **Margaret Riley.** 23a PP. RILEY 1966. Award of Merit.
Tight incurved form. Broad pale pink florets that build up to give a globular bloom. Height approx. 3 ft 6 in. – September.

116 **Marilyn Gates.** 23b PY. PATILLA/JOHNSON 1966. Award of Merit.
Tightly incurved. Canary yellow florets that close over at the top to give a globular bloom. Small dark green foliage. Height approx. 3 ft 6 in. – September.

117 **Evelyn Bush.** 25a W. SHOESMITH/THISTLETHWAITE 1955.
Incurving form. Broad white florets that build up to give a solid bloom of great merit. Height approx. 4 ft – September.

118 **Nancy Matthews.** 23b W. MATTHEWS/STEVENSON 1961.
Tight incurved form. The neat white florets overlap gracefully to give a completely ball-shaped bloom. Height approx. 3 ft 6 in. – September.

119 **Martin Riley.** 23b Y. RILEY 1961.
A fine bright golden yellow incurved bloom of perfect globular shape. Small neat foliage. Height approx. 3 ft – September.

120 **Stephen Rowe.** 23b Y. ROWE 1970.
Incurved form. Narrow rolled florets of bright yellow with old-gold reverse. Full centred bloom. Neat foliage. Height approx. 4 ft – September.

121 **Pat Amos.** 23a W. PATILLA/JOHNSON 1967. Preliminary Commendation.
An exceptionally large flowered white incurve with broad florets. The bloom is almost too heavy for the stem. Most suitable for exhibition purposes. Height approx. 5 ft – September.

122 **Primrose Ermine.** 23a PY. ROWE 1964. Sport from Ermine.
Classical incurved form. Broad florets of true primrose yellow colour. A good flower for the exhibitor. Height approx. 3 ft 6 in. – September.

123 **Ruth Standley.** 23a W. STANDLEY 1970. Preliminary Commendation.
Classical incurved form. Creamy white broad florets of good texture. Good blooms and neat foliage. Height approx. 3 ft 6 in. – September.

124 **Susan Mary.** 23a PP. GURR/WILSON 1969.
Incurved form. Broad purple-pink florets with just enough length to give a globular bloom. Height approx. 3 ft 6 in. – September.

125 **Jane Riley.** 23a W. RILEY 1970. Award of Merit.
Finishes to a perfect incurve of exceptional size. Broad white crisp florets. Very vigorous growth. A flower for the exhibitor. Height approx. 4 ft – September.

126 **Yellow Nugget** 23b Y. SHOESMITH 1964. Award of Merit.
A true incurve of excellent form. Broad butter yellow florets of good texture.

Dark green foliage. Height approx. 4 ft
4 in – September.

127 **Ernest Avison** 23a W. JOHNSON
1970. Preliminary Commendation.
Broad white florets which finish perfectly to give a globular bloom of classical form. Dwarf habit. Height approx.
3 ft – September.

128 **Anna Marie** 19c W. HOEK/WALKER
1969.
Reflexing white spray Upright stems
carrying clusters of glistening flowers.
Compact habit. Height approx. 3 ft 3 in.
Flowering period, August and September.

129 **Salmon Pye** 29d R. ELMHOUSE 1966.
Single type salmon red spray. Upright
stems. Clusters of very decorative
flowers. Compact habit. Height approx.
3 ft. Flowering period, August and
September.

130 **Solley.** 29c Y. EMMANS 1960.
Reflexed yellow spray, Dwarf habit.
Compact plants. Very prolific. Height
approx. 21 in. Flowering period, August
and September.

131 **Hunstanton.** 28b P. ELMHOUSE
1967.
Pompon spray type. Upright stems
carrying clusters of rosy pink flowers.
Vigorous growth. Height approx 3 ft
6 in. Flowering period, August and
September.

132 **Alan.** 28a R. CAUNT/JOHNSON 1961.
Dwarf pompon type. Low bushy plants
with a profusion of deep crimson
flowers. Height approx. 14 in. Flowering period, August and September.

133 **Lemon Tench.** 29d Y. ELMHOUSE
1966.
Single spray type. Very dwarf compact

bushy plants carrying masses of lemon
yellow flowers over a long period.
Height approx. 14 in. – July, August
and September.

134 **Pinocchio.** 29c LB. HOLLAND/ELM-
HOUSE 1965.
Reflexing spray type. Tall upright stems
carrying clusters of light copper bronze
flowers. Height approx. 4 ft. – August
and September.

135 **Pamela.** 29c B. HOEK/WALKER 1969.
Reflexing spray type. Upright grower.
Compact plant carrying clusters of rich
copper bronze flowers. Good foliage.
Height approx. 3 ft – August and
September.

136 **Poppet.** 28a Y. SHOESMITH 1951.
Award of Merit.
Grown as a spray. Blooms are of pompon type. Upright stems carrying
clusters of bright golden ball-shaped
flowers. Height approx. 2 ft 9 in. –
August and September.

137 **Fairie.** 28a P. JOHNSON 1956.
Pompon-shaped flowers. Very dwarf
compact plants. Vigorous growth. Free
flowering. Plants carry a profusion of
salmon pink ball-shaped flowers.
Height approx. 16 in. – August and
September.

138 **Winkie.** 28 Y. JOHNSON 1958.
Pompon-shaped flowers. Compact upright growth. Having clusters of flowers
of bright yellow shading to bronze in the
centre. Height approx. 2 ft 6 in. –
August and September.

139 **Lucida.** 29c Y. HOLLAND/ELMHOUSE
1965.
Reflexing maize yellow spray type. Upright stems carrying clusters of weatherproof flowers. Height approx. 3 ft –
August and September.

140 Premier. 26 Y. NAPIER'S 1952. Award of Merit.

Anemone-centred type. Golden yellow ray florets with pale yellow dome-shaped cushion in the centre. Free flowering. Upright stems. Height approx. 4 ft – September.

141 Aurora Queen. 29c R. ELMHOUSE 1966.

Reflexing spray. Upright stems carrying clusters of scarlet flowers with bronze centre florets. Height approx. 2 ft 6 in. – August and September.

142 Madeleine Queen. 29c P. ELMHOUSE 1966.

Reflexing spray type. Compact habit. Good foliage. Upright stems carrying masses of soft shell pink flowers with centre cushion of florets blending to a deeper shade. Height approx. 3 ft 6 in. – August and September.

143 Adelaine Queen. 29c W. HOLLAND/H. WALKER 1967.

Reflexing spray type. Compact and vigorous growth. Upright stems carrying clusters of glistening white flowers that have a yellowish green tinge in the centre. Height approx. 3 ft – August and September.

144 Charming. 29c PP. ROWE 1961. Award of Merit.

Reflexing spray type. Compact, vigorous and upright growth. Good length of stem carrying a well balanced spray of shell pink flowers. Height approx. 3 ft 6 in. – September.

145 Clarette Queen. 29c W. HOLLAND/ELMHOUSE 1968.

Reflexing spray type. Compact vigorous growth. Good stems. Neat foliage providing a pleasant foil to the attractive white flowers which are enhanced by lemon yellow centres. Height approx. 3 ft – September.

146 Sweetness. 28b P. JOHNSON 1961.

Pompon. The tubular type florets build up to make a bloom of globular shape. Stiff stems furnished with neat foliage. The flowers are a pastel shade of pink which is intensified in the centres. Height approx. 2 ft 6 in. – September.

147 Lilian Hoek. 29c B. HOEK/ELMHOUSE 1964. Award of Merit.

Reflexing spray type. Upright growth. Stiff stems carrying 4–5 blooms approximately $2\frac{1}{2}$ in. in diameter. The centre cushion of florets mid-bronze shading to light bronze at full development. Height approx. 2 ft 9 in. – August and September.

(ii) OCTOBER-FLOWERING, MID-SEASON AND LATE-FLOWERING CHRYSANTHEMUMS

148 Fantastic. 16 W. SHOESMITH 1961. Award of Merit.
Very large October-flowering. This section has been developed from the mid-season Large Exhibition type. The plants will carry three well developed blooms up to 7 in. in diameter. The broad pure white florets give a bloom of globular outline (there is also a pale yellow sport). Can be grown in the open ground but needs overhead protection at flowering time. Height approx. 4 ft – September–October.

149 Fairglow. 15b LB. ROWE 1969. Preliminary Commendation.
Incurving form. Inner florets rich orange bronze with light bronze reverse. Good stems and neat foliage. Requires overhead or greenhouse protection at flowering time. Height approx. 4 ft 6 in. – October.

150 Pinklea. 15a P. ROWE 1968. Preliminary Commendation.
Incurving form. Rose pink inner florets with silver reverse of good texture and lasting quality. Well balanced foliage. Overhead or greenhouse protection at flowering time. Height approx. 4 ft 6 in. – October.

151 Jennifer Squires. 14b P. SHOESMITH/JEFFERIES 1967. Award of Merit.
Classical reflexed form. The blooms have good shoulders and depth. Broad cyclamen pink florets. Overhead or greenhouse protection at flowering time. Height approx. 4 ft – October.

152 Carousel. 15a PP. ROWE 1963.
Incurving form. Broad pale pink inner florets with silver pink reverse. Stiff stems. Neat foliage. Overhead or greenhouse protection at flowering time. Height approx. 4 ft 6 in. – October.

153 Copeland. 14b P. ROWE 1969.
Reflexing form. Broad pink florets with salmon tinge that overlap gracefully to give a neat compact bloom. Overhead or greenhouse protection at flowering time. Height approx. 4 ft – October.

154 Coverack. 14b B. ROWE 1969.
Reflexing form. Rich copper bronze florets of good substance. Overhead or greenhouse protection at flowering time. Height approx. 4 ft – October.

155 Glen Rosa. 13b Pu. ROWE 1969.
True incurved form. Broad florets that build up to give a globular bloom. Inner florets rich purple with a blue-purple reverse. Overhead or greenhouse protection at flowering time. Height approx. 4 ft – October.

156 Moorland. 15b B. ROWE 1969.
Incurving form. Rich bronze inner florets with mid-bronze reverse. Upright growth. Neat foliage. Overhead or greenhouse protection at flowering time. Height approx. 4 ft – October.

157 Brompton. 5a P. ROWE 1967. Award of Merit.
Incurving form. Florets rich rosy pink with silver reverse. Small neat foliage. Height approx. 4 ft 6 in. – October–November under glass.

158 Western Tints. 15a LB. ROWE 1970. Preliminary Commendation.
Incurving form. Broad hard orange-bronze florets with gold reverse. Dark green foliage. Overhead or greenhouse protection at flowering time. Height approx. 4 ft – October.

159 Woolman's Yellow. 1 Y. WOOLMAN 1967. Preliminary Commendation.

Large Exhibition. A solid bloom with canary yellow neatly reflexing hard crisp florets. Height approx. 4 ft 6 in. Grown in pots in the open and flowered under glass in November.

160 Cheddar. 13a Y. ROWE 1968. Award of Merit.

Classified as October flowering, this very attractive chrysanthemum can be flowered late in September, through October and early November. It has classic incurved form. The butter yellow florets give a bloom of perfect globular shape, the only weakness being the tendency to spot at the base. Height approx. 5 ft.

161 Harry Gee. 1 PP. WOOLMAN 1967. Preliminary Commendation.

Large Exhibition. An almost perfect reflexed bloom. Long beautiful silvery pink florets. Good healthy growth. Dwarf and compact habit. Height 3 ft 6 in. Grown in pots in the open and flowered under glass in November.

162 James Bryant. 1 R. BRYANT/WOOLMAN 1935.

Large Exhibition. The best red in this section. Long broad chestnut crimson florets with gold tips. A very solid bloom with full centre. Dark green foliage. Height approx. 5 ft 6 in. Grown in pots in the open and flowered under glass in November.

163 Jessie Habgood. 1 W. WOOLMAN 1948.

Large Exhibition. Large well shouldered bloom. Long broad white florets that reflex gracefully to make an attractive flower of good substance. Height approx. 5 ft 6 in. Grown in pots in the open and flowered under glass in November.

164 Lilac Prince. 1 P. WOOLMAN 1954.

Large Exhibition. Very large well shouldered bloom. Broad pale pink florets that interlace or whorl in their reflexing form. Height approx. 4 ft 6 in. Grown in pots in the open and flowered under glass in November.

165 Edith Woolman. 1 P. WOOLMAN 1942. First Class Certificate.

Large Exhibition. Classical reflexed form. Broad salmon pink florets, full in the centre. Immaculate form. Height approx. 4 ft. Grown in pots in the open and flowered under glass in November.

166 Mark Woolman. 1 Y. WOOLMAN 1958. First Class Certificate.

Large Exhibition. A magnificent flower of large size. Rich yellow florets interlace and whorl as they build up a bloom of incurving form. Height approx. 5 ft. Grown in pots in the open and flowered under glass in November.

167 Shirley Primrose syn **Patricia Barnett.** 1 Y. POCKETT/WOOLMAN 1940. First Class Certificate.

Large Exhibition. A giant sized flower with long broad lemon yellow florets that interlace and whorl to give a magnificent bloom of incurving formation. Height approx. 5 ft 6 in. Grown in pots in the open and flowered under glass in November.

168 Keith Luxford. 1 P. BRYANT/LUXFORD 1948. First Class Certificate.

Large Exhibition. Traditional incurving formation that reveals the inner colour of the purplish pink broad florets and reflects a pale mauve silver pink reverse. Very hard florets of good texture. Height approx. 5 ft. Grown in pots in the open and flowered under glass in November.

169 **Rita Jones.** 1 W. FURNEAUX OF AUSTRALIA/ROYLES 1968. Award of Merit.

Large Exhibition. Incurving form. The broad white florets interlace and whorl as they build up to give a bloom of globular outline. Height approx. 5 ft 6 in. Grown in pots in the open and flowered under glass in November.

170 **Ruby Edwards.** 1 LB. PEPPER 1964. Sport from George Edwards.

Large Exhibition. Incurving form. The long broad florets are golden yellow on the inside, the reverse showing a pronounced reddish lilac as they interlace and whorl to give a bloom of globular outline. Height approx. 6 ft. Grown in pots in the open and flowered under glass in November.

171 **Shirley Champion.** 1 Y. POCKETT/WOOLMAN 1948.

Large Exhibition. Incurving form. Deep yellow broad florets that interlace and whorl giving a solid bloom of globular outline. Height approx. 5 ft 6 in. Grown in pots in the open and flowered under glass in November.

172 **Primrose Jessie Habgood.** 1 Y. WOOLMAN 1956. Award of Merit. Sport from Jessie Habgood.

Large Exhibition. Very large well shouldered bloom. Long broad pale yellow florets that reflex gracefully to make an attractive flower of good substance. Height approx. 5 ft 6 in. Grown in pots in the open and flowered under glass in November.

173 **Woking Rose.** 1 P. SHOESMITH 1963. Award of Merit.

Large Exhibition. Traditional incurving form which reveals the inner colour of the deep rose pink florets reflecting a silvery pink reverse. A very sturdy grower. Height approx. 4 ft. Grown in pots in the open and flowered under glass in November.

174 **George Edwards.** 1 PP. WOOLMAN 1945. First Class Certificate.

Large Exhibition. Incurving form. The long broad pale lilac florets interlace and whorl to make a bloom of globular outline. Height approx. 6 ft. Grown in pots in the open and flowered under glass in November.

175 **Cream Duke.** 1 PY. DALE 1948. Sport from Duke of Kent.

Large Exhibition. Reflexed form. Long rolled deep cream florets that overlap gracefully to give a solid bloom of immense size. Height approx. 5 ft 6 in. Grown in pots in the open and flowered under glass in November.

176 **Gigantic.** 1 S. SHOESMITH 1962.

Large Exhibition. Incurving form. Long broad salmon bronze florets with silvery pink reverse that interlace and whorl to build up to a huge bloom of globular outline. Vigorous habit. Height approx. 5 ft 6 in. Grown in pots in the open and flowered under glass in November.

177 **J. S. Dakers.** 1 P. LUXFORD/DALE 1950. Award of Merit.

Large Exhibition. Reflexed form. Long rolled pale pink florets with a bluish tinge that overlap gracefully to make a fully reflexing bloom. Height approx. 5 ft 6 in. Grown in pots in the open and flowered under glass in November.

178 **Pamela Williams.** 1 W. WOOLMAN 1967. Award of Merit.

Large Exhibition. A well shouldered bloom of good depth. Reflexing form. Pure white florets. Height approx. 4ft. Grown in pots in the open and flowered under glass in November.

179 **Amethyst.** 1 Pu. WOOLMAN 1949. First Class Certificate.

Large Exhibition. Well shouldered bloom of classical reflexed form. The amethyst-rose florets reflect a paler tint on the reverse, overlapping gracefully to make a most attractive flower. Height approx. 4 ft 6 in. Grown in pots in the open and flowered under glass in November.

180 **Monica Bennett.** 1 P. SHOESMITH 1964.

Large Exhibition. Rich clear pink. Fully reflexing form. Healthy vigorous growth, producing a solid bloom with full centres. Height approx. 4 ft 6 in. Grown in pots in the open and flowered under glass in November.

181 **Shirley Giant.** 1 P. WOOLMAN 1964. Award of Merit.

Large Exhibition. Incurving form. Florets cerise on the inside with a silvery pink reverse. They interlace and whorl to give a large bloom of globular form. Height approx. 5 ft. Grown in pots in the open and flowered under glass in November.

182 **Red Majestic.** 1 R. JONES 1925. Sport from Majestic.

Large Exhibition. Classical reflexed form. Broad terra cotta florets overlap gracefully to give a bloom with good shoulders and depth. Height 4 ft 6 in. Grown in pots in the open and flowered under glass in November.

183 **Betty Barnes.** 1 LB. WOOLMAN 1951. First Class Certificate.

Large Exhibition. Reflexing form. Broad pale apricot florets that interlace and whorl to give a bloom with good shoulders and depth. Height approx. 5 ft. Grown in pots in the open and flowered under glass in November.

184 **Duke Of Kent.** 1 W. POCKETT/WOOLMAN 1938. Award of Merit.

Large Exhibition. Reflexing form. Very long drooping off-white florets that build up to make a very large bloom with broad shoulders and great depth. Height approx. 5 ft 6 in. Grown in pots in the open and flowered under glass in November.

185 **Connie Mayhew.** 2 Y. WANTANABI/WOOLMAN/LUXFORD 1951.

Medium Exhibition. Classical incurved form. Broad smooth pale yellow florets with sufficient length to enable them to incurve gracefully to give a bloom of globular outline. Height approx. 5 ft. Grown in pots in the open and flowered under glass in November.

186 **Cossack.** 2 R. WOOLMAN 1943. First Class Certificate.

Medium Exhibition. Classical reflexed form. Deep crimson florets with velvet sheen. They overlap gracefully to make an immaculate bloom. Dark green foliage. Height 4 ft 6 in. Grown in pots in the open and flowered under glass in November.

187 **Golden Wedding.** 2 Y. WOOLMAN 1963. Award of Merit.

Medium Exhibition. Incurving form. Rich shining golden yellow florets that interlace and whorl to give a bloom of globular outline. Height 4 ft. Grown in pots in the open and flowered under glass in November.

188 **Rita Shirley.** 2 P. WOOLMAN 1957. Award of Merit.

Medium Exhibition. Incurving form. broad lilac pink florets that make up a solid bloom of globular outline. Vigorous habit. Height 4 ft 6 in. Grown in pots in the open and flowered under glass in November.

189 **Audrey Shoesmith.** 3a P. SHOE-
SMITH 1956. First Class Certificate.
Exhibition Incurved. True incurved
form. Florets are pale pink at the base
shading to warm white at the tips.
Perfect globular form, hard texture.
Height 5 ft 6 in. Grown in pots in the
open and flowered under glass in
November.

190 **Frances Jefferson.** 3b LB. WOOLMAN
1963. Award of Merit.
Exhibition Incurved. True incurved
form. Florets clear amber bronze. Hard
texture, small foliage which is a neat foil
to a medium-sized flower. Height 4 ft
6 in. Grown in pots in the open and
flowered under glass in November.

191 **Dexta.** 3a Y. RILEY 1963. Award of
Merit.
Exhibition Incurved. The closely laid
bright yellow florets incurve to make a
bloom of near perfect globular shape.
Neat foliage making a well balanced
plant. Height 4 ft. Grown in pots in the
open and flowered under glass in
November.

192 **Dorridge Cream.** 3a PY. WOOLMAN
1967. Award of Merit. (See also illustration **267**).
Exhibition Incurved. True incurved
form. Pale yellow florets with creamy
reverse that incurve gracefully to give a
globular bloom. Dwarf habit. Height 3
ft 6 in. Grown in pots in the open and
flowered under glass in November.

193 **John Rowe.** 3a Y. ROWE 1961.
Award of Merit.
Exhibition Incurved. Broad bright
yellow cupped florets that build up to a
tightly incurved solid bloom. Easy to
grow, good habit, dark green foliage.
Height 4 ft. Grown in pots in the open
and flowered under glass in November.

194 **Langley.** 3b Y. ROWE 1967. Award
of Merit.
Exhibition Incurved. The blooms are
tightly incurved, rich yellow in colour.
Possesses excellent keeping qualities,
good habit, neat foliage. Height 4 ft.
Grown in pots in the open and flowered
under glass in November.

195 **Marjorie Montague.** 3b W. WOOL-
MAN 1968.
Exhibition Incurved. The habit and
growth are good, carries an even crop of
exhibition quality blooms. The solid
white florets do not pink at the base.
compact habit. Height 4 ft 6 in. Grown
in pots in the open and flowered under
glass in November.

196 **Mary Ann Royles.** 3a Y. WILSON/
ROYLES 1969. Preliminary Commendation.
Exhibition Incurved. Rich butter yellow
florets of good texture that build up to
give a classical and very hard textured
incurved bloom. Neat foliage. Height
4 ft 6 in. Grown in pots in the open and
flowered under glass in November.

197 **Mavis Shoesmith.** 3a P. SHOESMITH
1962. Award of Merit.
Exhibition Incurved. Broad smooth
mauve pink florets with sufficient length
to enable them to curve gracefully to
give a bloom completely globular in
outline. The regular placement of the
florets make a bloom of classical form.
Height 5 ft. Grown in pots in the open
and flowered under glass in November.

198 **Minstrel Boy.** 3b LB. SHOESMITH
1963. (See also **265**).
Exhibition Incurved. One of the classics
in this section. Golden bronze florets
toning to a deeper shade at the base.
Finishes to a completely globular solid
bloom. Small foliage. An exhibitor's

flower. Height 4 ft 6 in. Grown in pots in the open and flowered under glass in November.

199 Maylen. 3b W. SHOESMITH 1957. Award of Merit.

Exhibition Incurved. Broad smooth ivory white florets. Strong constitution, excellent dark green foliage. An exhibitor's flower, or will carry a good crop for cut flower work. Height 4 ft. Grown in pots in the open and flowered under glass in November.

200 Severn. 3b LB. SHOESMITH/JEFFERIES 1967. Award of Merit.

Exhibition Incurved. Light coffee bronze florets. Very hard texture to give it good keeping qualities. Very vigorous growth, compact habit, small foliage. Height 4 ft 6 in. Grown in pots in the open and flowered under glass in November.

201 Shirley Imp. 3b S. WOOLMAN 1969. Preliminary Commendation.

Exhibition Incurved. Salmon bronze florets of good texture that make a solid hard bloom. Every flower good, resistant to damping, compact habit. Height 4 ft. Grown in pots in the open and flowered under glass in November.

202 Shirley Model. 1 R. WOOLMAN 1964. Award of Merit. (See also illustration **270**).

Exhibition Incurved. Broad mauve purple florets that build up to make a perfect ball shaped bloom. Very hard and reliable, good dark green foliage. Height 4 ft. Grown in pots in the open and flowered under glass in November.

203 Waterloo. 3b B. ROWE 1964. Award of Merit.

Exhibition Incurved. Rich bronze florets that tone to a golden bronze at the tips. A very distinctive reddish reverse giving a bi-coloured effect. Hard-petalled and reliable. Dark green foliage. Height 4 ft. Grown in pots in the open and flowered under glass in November.

204 Dorothy Whittock. 3b O. SHOESMITH/JEFFERIES 1969.

Exhibition Incurved. The form is so perfect it is hard to omit from a collection of true incurves. In the early stages of bloom development there is considerable colour variation which disappears as the bloom reaches its peak and becomes an off-white shade. Vigorous habit, good foliage. Height 4 ft 6 in. Grown in pots in the open and flowered under glass in November.

205 Golden Maylen. 3b Y. HEYWOOD 1962. Sport from Maylen.

Exhibition Incurved. Broad smooth golden yellow florets. Strong constitution, excellent dark green foliage. An exhibitor's flower or will carry a good crop for cut flower work. Height 4 ft. Grown in pots in the open and flowered under glass in November.

206 Red Shirley Model. 3a O. WOOLMAN 1967. Preliminary Commendation. Sport from Shirley Model. (See also illustration **269**).

Exhibition Incurved. The same type of flower and habit as its parent. Broad wine red florets with rich copper bronze reverse. Height 3 ft 6 in. Grown in pots in the open and flowered under glass in November.

207 Woolman's Perfecta. 3a W. WOOLMAN 1963. Award of Merit.

Exhibition Incurved. Broad long white florets that build up to give a bloom of egg shaped outline. There are plenty of petals to make a very solid flower. Good foliage. Height 5 ft. Grown in pots in the open and flowered under glass in November.

208 **Edward Rowe.** 3b Y. ROWE 1970.
Exhibition Incurved. Deep butter yellow florets. Extremely hard texture, finishes well, good dark green foliage. Height 4 ft. Grown in pots in the open and flowered under glass in November.

209 **Ron Shoesmith.** 3b W. SHOESMITH 1963. First Class Certificate.
Exhibition Incurved. Hard white florets gracefully incurving to give a completely ball shaped bloom of extremely hard texture. Good foliage. Height 4 ft. Grown in pots in the open and flowered under glass in November.

210 **Vera Woolman.** 3b Y. WOOLMAN 1953. First Class Certificate.
Exhibition Incurved. Clear yellow florets with a green tinge towards the centre. Very hard texture giving long lasting qualities. Neat foliage. Height 4 ft. Grown in pots in the open and flowered under glass in November.

211 **Shirley Empress.** 3a Y. WOOLMAN 1970.
Although classified as an Incurved, the florets do not close completely at the top. Best described as 'Incurving'. Very good hard bloom, compact habit. Height 4 ft 6 in. Grown in pots in the open and flowered under glass in November.

212 **Brett Williams.** 3b Y. SHOESMITH/JEFFERIES 1970.
Exhibition Incurved. Broad deep yellow florets of good texture. Plants are vigorous in habit giving a crop of uniform flowers. Height 5 ft 6 in. Grown in pots in the open and flowered under glass in November.

213 **Goldkist.** 13b Y. ROWE 1965. Preliminary Commendation.
Exhibition Incurved. Broad Rich golden yellow florets. Compact habit, neat foliage. Gives a good crop for cut flower or exhibition work. Height 4 ft 6 in. Grown in pots in the open and flowered under glass in October and November.

214 **Woolman's Temptation.** 3b PP. WOOLMAN 1970. Preliminary Commendation.
An attractive pale pink Incurved. Neat compact bloom of hard texture. Height 4 ft 6 in. Grown in pots in the open and flowered under glass in November.

215 **Yellow Ron Shoesmith.** 3b Y. BROWNSLAND 1958. Sport from Ron Shoesmith.
Exhibition Incurved. Butter yellow florets that gracefully incurve to give a completely ball shaped bloom of extremely hard texture. Good foliage. Height 4 ft. Grown in pots in the open and flowered under glass in November.

216 **Flashpoint.** 4b R. ROWE 1969. Award of Merit.
Reflexed form. Rich crimson florets with gold tips. Compact habit, dark green foliage. Good cut flower type. Height 4 ft 6 in. Grown in pots in the open and flowered under glass in November.

217 **Halloween.** 4b R. RILEY 1965. Award of Merit.
Reflexed form. Rich red florets with gold reverse. Vigorous habit and will carry a good crop for cutting or exhibition. Height 4 ft. Grown in pots in the open and flowered under glass in October and November.

218 **London Gazette.** 4b R. SHOESMITH/JEFFERIES 1967. Award of Merit.
Reflexed form. Crimson red florets with gold reverse. Very full centres, upright habit, dark green foliage. Height 4 ft 6

in. Grown in pots in the open and flowered under glass in November.

219 Elizabeth Deeley. 4a P. HALL 1969. Preliminary Commendation.

Rich carnation pink Reflexed of good form. The florets retain their colour well with very little fading. Height 4 ft. Grown in pots in the open and flowered under glass in November.

220 Apricot My Lady. 4b S. WOOLMAN 1956. Sport from My Lady.

Medium-flowered. Immaculate reflexed form. Salmon pink florets that overlap gracefully to give a very neat and refined finish. Compact habit, good foliage. Height 4 ft. Grown in pots in the open and flowered under glass in November.

221 Polar Gem. 3a W. SHOESMITH/ JEFFERIES 1967. Award of Merit. (See also illustration **264**).

Exhibition Incurved. The white florets have a greenish tinge. Being very crisp they are free from damping. The bloom is conical rather than ball shaped in outline. Height 4 ft 6 in. Grown in pots in the open and flowered under glass in November.

222 Primrose Mona Davis. 4a PY. COTTAM 1968. Preliminary Commendation. Sport from Mona Davis.

One of several sports from the parent. Stocks available today have been revitalised by heat treatment as the original was introduced in 1904. The form is classically reflexed and the primrose florets are tinged with apricot. Compact habit, good foliage. Height 4 ft. Grown in pots in the open and flowered under glass in November.

223 Stuart Shoesmith. 4a LB. SHOESMITH 1961. Award of Merit.

Reflexed form. Glowing amber bronze florets, the centre cushion tinged with green. Upright habit, stiff stems, good foliage. Height 4 ft 6 in. Grown in pots in the open and flowered under glass in November.

224 Walker's Jewel. 4a PP. WALKER 1968. Preliminary Commendation.

Reflexed form. Broad pearl pink florets that overlap gracefully in the classical reflexed style. Upright habit, good foliage. Height 5ft 6in. Grown in pots in the open and flowered under glass in November.

225 Capri. 4b Pu. SHOESMITH/JEFFERIES 1970. Preliminary Commendation.

Reflexed classical formation and unusual colour of rich purple pink. The more mature florets show a slight whitish colouration near the tips which add to its charm. A good solid bloom, upright habit. Height 4 ft 6 in. Grown in pots in the open and flowered under glass in November.

226 Deep Pink Joy Hughes. 4b P. WALKER 1966. Preliminary Commendation. Sport from Joy Hughes.

The deep rose pink florets are fully reflexing. They are narrow, rolled and of spiky formation. When mature they last well both on the plant and when used for floral decoration. Good foliage. Height 4 ft. Grown in pots in the open and flowered under glass in November.

227 Joy Hughes. 4b P. SHOESMITH 1960. Award of Merit.

The carnation pink florets are fully reflexing. They are narrow, rolled and of spiky formation. When mature they last well both on the plant and when used for floral decoration. Good foliage. Height 4 ft. Grown in pots in the open and flowered under glass in November.

228 Yellow Princess Anne. 4b Y. R. C. SMITH 1957. Preliminary Commendation. Sport from Princess Anne.

Reflexing form. Clear yellow florets of good texture. All the Princess Anne family are compact and vigorous in growth with good clean foliage. The plants will always give a reliable crop of flowers. Height 3 ft 6 in. Grown in pots in the open and flowered under glass in November.

229 **Apricot Princess Anne.** 4b LB. VALENTINE 1955. Award of Merit. Sport from Princess Anne.
Reflexing form. Deep yellow florets tinged with apricot. All the Princess Anne family are compact and vigorous in growth with good clean foliage. The plants will always give a reliable crop of flowers. Height 3 ft 6 in. Grown in pots in the open and flowered under glass in November.

230 **Princess Anne.** 4b P. SHOESMITH 1951. Award of Merit.
Attractive flushed salmon florets of reflexing form. The plants are healthy, vigorous and of compact habit producing a good crop of flowers with good foliage. This cultivar, and its sports, is used extensively for commercial work as cut flowers and dwarf pot plants. Height 4 ft. Grown in pots in the open and flowered under glass in November.

231 **Crimson Lake.** 4a R. SHOESMITH 1954. Award of Merit.
Reflexed form. The rich crimson florets have a velvet sheen. They overlap gracefully to give a classical bloom. Good dark green foliage. Height 5 ft. Grown in pots in the open and flowered under glass in November.

232 **Copper Globe.** 5b LB. BELL 1965.
Incurving form. Light bronze florets with deep bronze reverse. Gives a good crop of globular shaped blooms on erect stems. Light green foliage.

Height 4 ft. Grown in pots in the open and flowered under glass in November.

233 **Bridal Gown.** 4a W. SHOESMITH 1963.
Classical reflexed form. Broad white pointed florets with pale peach shading. Strong growth, compact habit. Height 4 ft. Grown in pots in the open and flowered under glass in November.

234 **My Lady.** 4b P. SHOESMITH 1953. Award of Merit.
Reflexed form. Soft light pink florets shading to salmon. Compact habit, good foliage. Height 4 ft. Grown in pots in the open and flowered under glass in November.

235 **Chantilly.** 4a O. SHOESMITH/ JEFFERIES 1969.
Reflexed form. Florets are pale yellow with a peach tinge. One of the few pastel shades in this section. Upright growth. Height 6 ft. Grown in pots in the open and flowered under glass in November.

236 **Yellow Symbol.** 4a Y. BALDWIN 1958. Sport from Symbol.
Classical reflexed form. Deep golden yellow florets of good texture that overlap evenly to give a compact bloom. Upright growth. Height 5 ft 6 in. Grown in pots in the open and flowered under glass in November.

237 **Elizabeth Woolman.** 4a P. WOOLMAN 1962.
A large perfectly finished reflexed bloom. The lilac pink florets build up evenly to give a solid bloom. Dwarf compact habit. Height 3 ft. Grown in pots in the open and flowered under glass in November.

238 **State Fair.** 4b LB. SHOESMITH/JEFFERIES 1967.

A broad shouldered reflexing light bronze bloom with full centres. Possesses good keeping qualities. Height 5 ft 6 in. Grown in pots in the open and flowered under glass in November.

239 Shirley Garnet. 4b R. WOOLMAN 1949. Award of Merit.
Reflexed form. The florets are rich chestnut red of good texture. Has good keeping qualities. Compact habit, dark green foliage. Height 4 ft 6 in. Grown in pots in the open and flowered under glass in November.

240 Avenger. 14b B. ROWE 1969.
Reflexing form. Rich copper bronze florets. Upright habit, neat foliage, good lasting qualities. Excellent for cut flower work. Height 4 ft 6 in. Grown in pots in the open and flowered under glass in November.

241 Kingsway. 15b Pu. ROWE 1969.
Incurving form. The inner florets are rich purple with a silver reverse. Upright habit, neat foliage, good lasting qualities as a cut flower. Height 4 ft 6 in. Grown in pots in the open and flowered under glass in October and November.

242 James Bond. 15b R. ROWE 1965. Award of Merit.
Incurving form. The cup shaped blooms reveal the brilliant red inner florets that have a gold reverse. Excellent keeping qualities, compact habit, good foliage. Height 4 ft. Grown in pots in the open and flowered under glass in October and November.

243 – 250 The **Mayford Perfection** family of chrysanthemums is one of the most popular of the late-flowering types. Originally introduced by the famous breeder, the late Harry Shoemith, the salmon-coloured parent has sported other attractive shades as illusrated. To obtain reflexed form they should be flowered on second crown buds. Growth of the plants is erect with good stiff stems and well balanced folige. The flowers are ideal for cut flower and decorative work. Height 5 ft.

243 Bronze Mayford Perfection. 4a B. BELL 1967. Sport from Mayford Perfection.
Reflexing form. Rich copper bronze florets. Grown in pots in the open and flowered under glass in November.

244 Red Mayford Perfection. 4a R. Sport from Mayford Perfection.
Reflexing form. Chestnut red florets. Grown in pots in the open and flowered under glass in November.

245 Primrose Mayford Perfection. 5a Y. ROWE 1960. Sport from Mayford Perfecion.
Reflexing form. Pale yellow florets. Grown in pots in the open and flowered under glass in November.

246 Yellow Mayford Perfection. 4a Y. Sport from Primrose Mayford perfection.
Reflexing form. Clear deep yellow florets. Grown in pots in the open and flowered under glass in November.

247 Mayford Perfection. 5a S. SHOE-SMITH 1954. Award of Merit.
Reflexing form. Pale salmon pink florets. Grown in pots in the open and flowered under glass in November.

248 Purple Mayford Perfection. 5a Pu. ROWE 1960. Sport from Mayford Perfection.
Reflexing form. Lilac pink florets. Grown in pots in the open and flowered under glass in November.

249 Dark Red Mayford Perfection. 4a R. Sport from Purple Mayford Perfection.

Reflexing form. Deep rich red florets. Grown in pots in the open and flowered under glass in November.

250 **Rose Mayford Perfection.** 5a P. ROWE 1957. Preliminary Commendation. Sport from Mayford Perfection.
Reflexing form. Bright rose pink florets. Grown in pots in the open and flowered under glass in November.

251 **Rylands Gold.** 14a LB. ROWE 1970.
Reflexed form. Broad rich bronze florets of good substance that build up to make a solid bloom carried on stiff stems. Good foliage. Ideal for cut flower and decorative work. Height 4 ft 6 in. Grown in pots in the open and flowered under glass in November.

252 **Doris Squires.** 5a PP. SHOE-SMITH/JEFFERIES 1968. Award of Merit.
Incurving form. A large flower of globular shape. Very hard pale pink florets that keep in good condition over a long period. Height 4 ft 6 in. Grown in pots in the open and flowered under glass in November.

253 **Cary Hodgson.** 5a Pu. SHOE-SMITH/JEFFERIES 1968. Preliminary Commendation.
Incurving form. Broad hard textured florets rich purple on the inside with silver-purple reverse. A good solid bloom carried on stiff stems. Neat dark green foliage. Height 4 ft 6 in. Grown in pots in the open and flowered under glass in November.

254 **Gold Foil.** 5a Y. WOOLMAN 1964.
Incurving form. Broad smooth clear shining yellow florets that build up to give a solid bloom of excellent quality. Stiff stems with good foliage. Must be grown from selected stock. Height 4 ft. Grown in pots in the open and flowered under glass in November.

255 **Watcombe.** 15b B. ROWE 1968. Award of Merit.
Incurving form. The cup shaped blooms reveal the inside colour of the florets, an attractive orange bronze with gold reverse. Compact habit, good foliage, an ideal plant for cut flower work. Height 4 ft 6 in. Grown in pots in the open and flowered under glass in November.

256 **Rose Shoesmith.** 5a P. SHOESMITH 1963. Award of Merit.
Although classified as an incurving type, the pale rose pink florets are of a very tight formation to make almost a true incurved. Strong vigorous growth, stiff stems, neat foliage. Height 4 ft. Grown in pots in the open and flowered under glass in November.

257 **Robert Shoesmith.** 5a W. SHOE-SMITH 1961.
A pure white chrysanthemum of incurving form. The broad florets build up to make a large globular bloom with a glistening sheen. Compact habit, stiff stems. Height 4 ft 6 in. Grown in pots in the open and flowered under glass in November.

258 **Olympic Queen.** 5a P. BELL 1968. Award of Merit.
Loosely incurving type which reveals the inner colour of the attractive rose pink florets that have a silver reverse. Blooms are carried on stiff stems. Dark green foliage, compact habit. Height 4 ft 6 in. Grown in pots in the open and flowered under glass in November.

259 **St. Moritz.** 5b W. ROWE 1967. Award of Merit.
Incurving form. Broad hard white florets give a bloom of good shape and quality. Compact habit, neat foliage. Height 4 ft 6 in. Grown in pots in the

open and flowered under glass in November.

260 John Markham. 5b Y. WOOLMAN 1968. Preliminary Commendation.
Loosely incurving form. Broad canary yellow florets of hard texture. Small foliage. A good cut flower type. Height 4 ft 6 in. Grown in pots in the open and flowered under glass in November.

261 Yellow Balcombe Perfection. 5a Y. BESSER/COLHAM GREEN 1962. Award of Merit. Sport from Balcombe Perfection.
Loosely incurving form, revealing the deep yellow of the inner florets which have a pale yellow reverse. Compact habit, vigorous growth, good foliage, ideal for cut flower work. Height 4 ft. Grown in pots in the open and flowered under glass in November.

262 Brenda Till. 5b PY. SHOESMITH/ JEFFERIES 1968.
Incurving form. Broad stiff florets that make up a cup shaped flower of excellent form. The inner florets are a pale creamy yellow with an even softer shade on the reverse. Stiff stems, good foliage. Height 5 ft. Grown in pots in the open and flowered under glass in November.

263 – 271 **Group:**

263 Mavis Shoesmith. 3a P. SHOESMITH 1962. Award of Merit.
True classical incurved. Broad smooth deep rose pink florets with a lilac tinge that build up to make a completely globular flower. Vigorous growth, stiff stems, good foliage. Height 5 ft. Grown in pots in the open and flowered under glass in November.

264 Polar Gem. 3a W. SHOESMITH/ JEFFERIES 1967. Award of Merit. (See **221**).

265 Minstrel Boy. 3b LB. SHOESMITH 1963.
Classical incurved form. Light golden bronze florets with a deeper shade at the base. Good upright habit, small foliage. Height 4 ft 6 in. Grown in pots in the open and flowered under glass in November.

266 Woking Perfection. 5b R. SHOESMITH 1954. Award of Merit.
Incurving form. Broad rich dark red florets with a bronze reverse. Good keeping qualities. Upright grower, dark green foliage, very reliable. Height 4 ft 6 in. Grown in pots in the open and flowered under glass in November.

267 Dorridge Cream. 3a PY. WOOLMAN 1967. Award of Merit. (See **192**).

268 Yellow Maylen. 3b Y. SHOESMITH/ HAYWOOD 1962. Sport from Maylen.
Classical incurved form. Broad smooth canary yellow florets. Good upright habit, fresh green foliage. Height 4 ft 6 in. Grown in pots in the open and flowered under glass in November.

269 Red Shirley Model. (See No. **206**).

270 Shirley Model. (See No. **202**).

271 Penguin. 4a W. SHOESMITH/ JEFFERIES 1968.
Reflexed form. Broad smooth pure white florets with pointed tips that overlap gracefully to give a compact bloom. Upright habit, dark green foliage. Height 4 ft. Grown in pots in the open and flowered under glass in November.

272 – 274 The **Balcombe Perfection** family of mid-season chrysanthemums is one of the most popular and reliable in this section. (See also **261**).

272 Balcombe Perfection. 5a B. SHOESMITH/VINTEN 1950. Award of Merit.

Loosely incurving form which reveals the inner orange bronze florets with light bronze reverse. Upright growth, excellent habit, good foliage. Height 4 ft. Grown in pots in the open and flowered under glass in November.

273 Amber Balcombe Perfection. 5a LB. COLHAM GREEN 1953. First Class Certificate. Sport from Balcombe Perfection.

Has the same characteristics as the parent. The inner florets are light amber with pale bronze reverse. Height 4 ft. Grown in pots in the open and flowered under glass in November.

274 Red Balcombe Perfection. 5a R. VINTEN/MAHER/GODBER 1951. First Class Certificate.

Probably the most popular of the Balcombe Perfection family due to the rich red colour of the inner florets reflecting a rich bronze on the reverse. Has all the good characteristics of the parent. Height 4 ft. Grown in pots in the open and flowered under glass in November.

275 Orange Fair Lady. 5a LB. ROWE 1966. Sport from Fair Lady.

A very attractive type of chrysanthemum. The lower florets reflex to reveal the inner colour of the broad orange bronze florets with the upper florets incurving to show the pale bronze reverse. Vigorous growth, heavy foliage. Height 4 ft. Grown in pots in the open and flowered under glass in November.

276 Leslie Tandy. 5a Pu. SHOESMITH 1958.

Tightly incurving form. Broad stiff florets rich purple on the inside with silver reverse. Upright growth, good lasting qualities. Height 4 ft. Grown in pots in the open and flowered under glass in November.

277 Lagoon. 5a P. SHOESMITH/JEFFERIES 1968. Award of Merit.

Classical incurving type with tight floret formation. Deep lilac on the inside with pale lilac reverse. The blooms of a hard texture producing good keeping qualities. Upright habit, good foliage. Height 4 ft 6 in. Grown in pots in the open and flowered under glass in November.

278 Sheridan. 5a B. SHOESMITH/JEFFERIES 1968. Preliminary Commendation.

Incurving form. Broad hard textured florets. Rich orange bronze on the inside with golden bronze reverse. Vigorous upright growth, good foliage, very attractive flower. Height 4 ft 6 in. Grown in pots in the open and flowered under glass in November.

279 Bronze Fair Lady. 5a B. ROWE 1965. Sport from Fair Lady.

Intermediate type of chrysanthemum. The lower florets reflex to reveal the inner colour of the golden bronze florets with the upper florets loosely incurving to show the pale bronze reverse. Vigorous grower, heavy foliage. Height 4 ft. Grown in pots in the open and flowered under glass in November.

280 Elizabeth Burton. 5a PP. WOOLMAN 1970. Preliminary Commendation.

Loosely incurving form. Broad florets an attractive shade of soft pale pink. Good type for cut flower and decorative work. Upright growth, good foliage. Height 5 ft. Grown in pots in the open and flowered under glass in November.

281 Group of Charms and Cascades.

This group of miniature chrysanthemums is very attractive, being used extensively for decorative work. They can be grown from seed sown during January and February and in subsequent seasons cuttings can be rooted during February and March. The Cascade type is similar, the trailing effect produced by a series of stoppings. See cultural notes on page 54. For further descriptions see **295, 296, 299** and **300.**

282 Mary Selvey. 4a R. SHOESMITH 1956. Award of Merit.

Classical reflexed form. The deep salmon red florets overlap evenly to give a compact and solid bloom. Upright habit, good foliage. Height 5 ft. Grown in pots in the open and flowered under glass in November.

283 Mary Jefferies. 5a W. SHOESMITH/ JEFFERIES 1967. Award of Merit.

Incurving form. Large broad creamy white florets of wax-like texture. The blooms are borne on strong upright stems. Very vigorous growth, large foliage. Needs to be well cropped for cut flower work. Height 5 ft 6 in. Grown in pots in the open and flowered under glass in November.

284 Fair Lady. 5a P. SHOESMITH 1959.

An attractive type of chrysanthemum. The lower florets reflex to reveal the inner colour of the broad pink florets with the upper florets incurving to show the pale pink reverse. Vigorous grower, heavy foliage. Height 4 ft. Grown in pots in the open and flowered under glass in November.

285 Gold Digger. 5a Y. RILEY 1966.

Incurving form. Broad stiff florets that make a cup-shaped bloom, golden yellow on the inside with butter yellow reverse. Upright habit, stiff stems, good foliage. Height 4 ft 6 in. Grown in pots in the open and flowered under glass in November.

286 Beacon. 5a R. SHOESMITH 1956.

Incurving form. Broad stiff wax-like florets that make a cup-shaped bloom revealing the rich crimson of the inner florets with golden bronze reverse. Vigorous habit, good stiff stems, dark green foliage. Height 4 ft 6 in. Grown in pots in the open and flowered under glass in November.

287 Thora. 6b P. CRAGG 1916.

Single type known as 'Anemone'. The cushion is the predominant feature from which the pink ray florets radiate to form an attractive flower. Very decorative. Upright habit, compact growth. Height 4 ft 6 in. Grown in pots in the open and flowered under glass in November.

288 Uranus. 7a R. SHOESMITH 1951. Award of Merit.

Single type having a centre disk of very short florets with up to five rows of ray florets. The disk is green when young, turning to yellow as the bloom matures. The ray florets are a rich red. Upright habit, neat dark green foliage. Height 4 ft. Grown in pots in the open and flowered under glass in November.

289 Daily Mirror. 5a Pu. SHOESMITH/ WOOLMAN 1965.

Tightly incurving type that builds up to a bloom of globular outline. Being slightly open in the centre it reveals the rich purple of the inner florets that have a silver reverse. Good upright habit, stiff stems, dark green foliage. Height 4 ft 6 in. Grown in pots in .the open and flowered under glass in November.

290 Copper Choice. 5b B. ROWE 1970. Preliminary Commendation.

Incurving form. Rich copper bronze florets that build up to give a refined symmetrical bloom. Upright habit, good stems and foliage. Height 4 ft 6 in. Grown in pots in the open and flowered under glass in November.

291 Harmony. 5a LB. SHOESMITH 1958. Incurving form. Stiff broad florets that give a cup shaped bloom revealing the orange bronze inner florets with gold reverse. Upright stems, compact habit, well balanced foliage. Height 4 ft 6 in. Grown in pots in the open and flowered under glass in November.

292 Elsie May. 7a LB. SHERWOOD 1967. Preliminary Commendation.
Single type. Centre disk green shading to gold. Ray florets light bronze. Upright habit, good stems, neat foliage. Height 4 ft. Grown in pots in the open and flowered under glass in November.

293 Edwin Painter. 7b Y. WOOLMAN 1961. Award of Merit.
Single type. Centre disk green shading to gold. Ray florets clear yellow. Dwarf compact habit. Stiff stems, neat foliage. Height 3 ft 6 in. Grown in pots in the open and flowered under glass in November.

294 Sunsilk. 7b LB. HALL 1967.
Single type. Centre disk green shading to gold. Ray florets rich golden yellow with silky sheen. Compact habit, upright stems, neat foliage. Height 4 ft. Grown in pots in the open and flowered under glass in November.

295 Pink Cascade. 11 P. SUTTON & SONS. (See also illustration **281**).
A type of chrysanthemum that has a branching habit with long wiry stems and deeply cut leaves. Carries masses of daisy like pink flowers approximately three-quarters of an inch in diameter. Grown in pots in the open and flowered under glass in November.

296 White Cascade. 11 W. SUTTON & SONS. (See also illustration **281**).
A type of chrysanthemum that has a branching habit with long wiry stems and deeply cut leaves. Carries masses of white daisy-like flowers approximately three-quarters of an inch in diameter. Grown in pots in the open and flowered under glass in November.

297 Chesswood Beauty. 7b R. H. LADDS/GREENYER 1935. Sport from Mason's Bronze.
Single type. Golden disk. Ray florets of rich crimson. Very neat compact bloom of perfect form. Upright habit, small neat foliage, very attractive. Height 4 ft. Grown in pots in the open and flowered under glass in November.

298 Marigold (Spray). 9c Y. U.S.A. Preliminary Commendation.
Spray type of chrysanthemum. Upright stems carrying clusters of golden yellow blooms $1\frac{1}{2}$ in. in diameter. Very decorative, ideal for floral arrangement. Height 4 ft. Grown in pots in the open and flowered under glass in November.

299 Yellow Charm. 11 Y. SUTTON & SONS. (See also illustration **281**).
Decorative pot plant grown from cutting. The plant forms a dome shape when fully developed carrying masses of single yellow flowers three-quarters of an inch in diameter. Grown in pots in the open and flowered under glass in November.

300 Red Charm. 11 R. SUTTON & SONS. (See also illustration **281**).
Decorative pot plant grown from cutting. The plant forms a dome shape

when fully developed, carrying masses of single red flowers three-quarters of an inch in diameter. Grown in pots in the open and flowered under glass in November.

301 **Woolman's Glory.** 7a B. WOOLMAN 1953. Award of Merit.
Single type. Golden yellow disk. Copper bronze ray florets which reflex at their tips. Upright habit, good stems, neat foliage. Height 4 ft 6 in. Grown in pots in the open and flowered under glass in November.

302 **Sun Valley.** 5a Y. SHOESMITH 1961. Award of Merit.
Incurving form. Broad clear yellow florets that incurve loosely to give a bloom of globular outline. Upright habit, stiff stems, dark green foliage. Height 5 ft. Grown in pots in the open and flowered under glass in November.

303 **Albert Cooper.** 7a Y. WOOLMAN 1949.
Single type. Clear yellow disk with green centre. Bright yellow ray florets. Upright habit, good stems, neat foliage. Height 4 ft 6 in. Grown in pots in the open and flowered under glass in November.

304 **Midlander.** 7a B. WOOLMAN 1965. Award of Merit.
Single type. Clear yellow disk with green centre. Ray florets rich copper bronze. Upright habit, dark green foliage. Height 4 ft. Grown in pots in the open and flowered under glass in November.

305 **Annina.** 7a Y. LUXFORD 1951.
Single type. Clear green disk. Ray florets straw yellow slightly flushed with pink. Tips of florets tend to incurve. Good foliage, upright growth. Height 5 ft. Grown in pots in the open and flowered under glass in November.

306 **Broadacre.** 7a W. WOOLMAN 1946. First Class Certificate.
Single type. Clear disk. Broad pure white ray florets that reflex at the tips. Dwarf habit. Height 3 ft. Grown in pots in the open and flowered under glass in November.

307 **Cleone.** 7a PP. GALVIN/LUXFORD 1936.
Single type. Immaculate form. Small green disk. Off-white ray florets that have a pale pink tinge at their tips. Upright habit, neat foliage. Height 5 ft. Grown in pots in the open and flowered under glass in November.

308 **Golden Woolman's Glory.** 7a Y. BACON 1962. Sport from Woolman's Glory.
Single type. Golden yellow disk. Golden amber ray florets that overlap evenly, reflexing at the tips. Upright habit, good foliage. Height 4 ft 6 in. Grown in pots in the open and flowered under glass in November.

309 **Nancy Sherwood.** 7b Y. SHERWOOD/WOOLMAN 1952. Award of Merit.
Single type. Clear green disk. Bright yellow ray florets. Very neat and compact plant, good foliage. Height 3 ft 6 in. Grown in pots in the open and flowered under glass in November.

310 **Preference.** 7a P. GREENYER 1955. Award of Merit.
Single type. Yellow disk with green centre. Ray florets pale pink shading to white where they radiate from the disk. There is a graceful curve in the horizontal line of the florets. Height 5 ft 6 in. Grown in pots in the open and flowered under glass in November.

311 **Jinx.** 7b W. LUXFORD 1943. First Class Certificate.

Single type. Clear green disk. Pure white pointed ray florets. Dwarf habit, thin stiff stems. Height 3 ft. Grown in pots in the open and flowered under glass in November.

312 Peggy Stevens. 7a Y. SHOESMITH/STUART OGG 1953. Award of Merit.

The largest single type at present in cultivation, yet a refined and attractive bloom. Large clear green disk, broad rich yellow florets. When well grown the blooms are 7–8 in. in diameter. Upright habit, good foliage. Height 4 ft. Grown in pots in the open and flowered under glass in November.

313 Red Woolman's Glory. 7a R. WOOLMAN 1960. Sport from Woolman's Glory.

Single type. Bright golden yellow disk. Rich chestnut red ray florets with reflexing tips. Upright habit, good stems. Height 4 ft 6 in. Grown in pots in the open and flowered under glass in November.

314 Yellow Cleone. 7a Y. WOOLMAN 1946. First Class Certificate. Sport from Cleone.

Single type. Immaculate form. Small green disk. Clear yellow ray florets. Upright habit, neat foliage. Height 5 ft. Grown in pots in the open and flowered under glass in November.

315 Fred Sherwood. 7a Pu. SHERWOOD 1970. Preliminary Commendation.

Single type. Immaculate form. Yellow disk with green centre. Ray florets cyclamen purple having a white tinge where they radiate from the disk. Upright habit, dark green foliage. Height 4 ft 6 in. Grown in pots in the open and flowered under glass in November.

316 Alice Fitton. 7b Pu. FITTON/BALDWIN 1964. Award of Merit.

Single type. Good form. Golden disk. Rich purple ray florets. Upright habit, dark green foliage. Height 4 ft 6 in. Grown in pots in the open and flowered under glass in November.

317 Alliance. 7b B. WOOLMAN 1967. Preliminary Commendation.

Single type. Bright golden disk. Pale orange bronze ray florets reflexing at the tips. Upright habit, dark green foliage. Height 4 ft. Grown in pots in the open and flowered under glass in November.

318 Rona (Single) 7b Pu. RAISER UNKNOWN.

Single type. Yellow disk with green centre. Ray florets cyclamen purple with a white tinge where they radiate from the disk. Upright habit, good foliage. Height 4 ft 6 in. Grown in pots in the open and flowered under glass in November.

319 Tokio. 10 W. RAISER UNKNOWN.

Spidery type. Quilled lace-like florets. White suffused with creamy green. Stiff wiry stems, small foliage. Ideal for floral arrangement. Height 4 ft 6 in. Grown in pots in the open and flowered under glass in November.

320 (a–h) Anemone Collection. 6a.

Very suitable for decorative and floral arrangement work. Easy to grow. Upright habit, thin wiry stems, small foliage. Height 4 ft 6 in. Grown in pots in the open and flowered under glass in November.

320a Brigida.

Cerise pink ray florets with silver-pink cushion.

320b Vivien.

Red ray florets with yellow cushion.

320c Tomaso.

Red ray florets with green and golden cushion.

320d **Oliviero.** Purple ray florets with green and silver cushion.

320e **Stefano.** White ray florets with pale yellow cushion.

320f **Basile.** Cream ray florets with amber cushion.

320g **Andre.** Light bronze ray florets with golden yellow cushion.

320h **Conrado.** Short bronze ray florets with large golden yellow cushion.

321 **Long Island Beauty.** 6a W. U.S.A./ LUXFORD 1947.
Anemone-centred type. Pale yellow cushion with green centre. Short white ray florets. Upright habit, stiff stems, small foliage. Very decorative. Height 4 ft. Grown in pots in the open and flowered under glass in November.

322 **Galaxy.** 9d B. U.S.A./COLHAM GREEN 1953. First Class Certificate.
Single type flowered in sprays. Green and gold centre disk. Bright orange bronze ray florets. Upright habit, stiff wiry stems, small foliage. Height 4 ft 6 in. Grown in pots in the open and flowered under glass in November.

323 **Red Rolinda.** 6b B. U.S.A./ENGEL-MAN 1939. First Class Certificate. Sport from Rolinda.
Anemone-centred type. Green and gold cushion. Rich chestnut bronze ray florets. Upright habit, stiff wiry stems, small foliage. Height 4 ft 6 in. Grown in pots in the open and flowered under glass in November.

324 **Yellow Galaxy.** 9d Y. sport from Galaxy.
Single type flowered in sprays. Green and yellow disk. Bright canary yellow ray florets. Upright habit, stiff wiry stems, small foliage. Height 4 ft. Grown in pots in the open and flowered under glass in November.

325 **Iceberg.** 9c W. U.S.A.
Decorative type flowered in sprays. Hard compact blooms. Lemon green centres shading to pure white. Upright habit, stiff wiry stems, small foliage. Height 4 ft. Grown in pots in the open and flowered under glass in November.

326 **Rayonnante Collection.** 10. Sports from Rayonnante.
Decorative and very popular with floral arrangers. Spidery formation, quilled florets. Stiff wiry stems, small foliage. Height 4 ft 6 in. Grown in pots in the open and flowered under glass in November.

326a **Bronze Rayonnante**

326b **Pink Rayonnante**

326c **White Rayonnante**

326d **Yellow Rayonnante**

326e **Rose Pink Rayonnante**

327 **Tuneful.** 9d B. RAISER UNKNOWN.
Single type flowered in sprays. Green and yellow disk. Bright orange bronze ray florets. Compact habit, stiff wiry stems, small foliage. Height 4 ft. Grown in pots in the open and flowered under glass in November.

328(a–g) **Spidery Collection.** 10.
Suitable for floral arrangements. Free growing. Stiff wiry stems, small foliage. Height 4 ft. Grown in pots in the open and flowered under glass in November.

328a **Cyrillus.** Pink quilled ray florets with green and golden-bronze cushion.

328b **Pietro.** Red-bronze ray florets with golden-yellow cushion.

328c **Edmundo.** Pink quilled spoon tipped ray florets with large silver-pink cushion.

328d **Magdalena.** Yellow quilled spoon tipped ray florets with golden-yellow cushion.

328e **Edgarus.** Golden-bronze quilled ray florets with green and bronze cushion.

328f **Theodorus.** Deep bronze with gold reverse ray florets with green and dark bronze cushion.

328g **White Spider.** White and pale pink quilled ray florets with yellow and green cushion.

329 **Shasta.** 9a W. U.S.A./MILLS 1963. Award of Merit.
Anemone-centred type flowered in sprays. Lemon yellow cushion, white ray florets. Stiff stems, small foliage. Height 4 ft. Grown in pots in the open and flowered under glass in November.

330 **Minstrel.** 9c P. COLHAM GREEN 1953. Small reflexing decorative type flowered in sprays. Compact rose pink florets, pale green centre. Stiff stems, dark green foliage. Height 4 ft. Grown in pots in the open and flowered under glass in November.

331 **Red Galaxy.** 9d R. U.S.A. Preliminary Commendation. Sport from Galaxy.
Single type flowered in sprays. Bright red ray florets, green and gold disk. Compact upright habit. Stiff stems, small foliage. Height 4 ft. Grown in pots in the open and flowered under glass in November.

332 **Yellow Galaxy.** 9d Y. sport from Galaxy. See No. 331.

333 **Tafetta.** 9c PP. U.S.A.
Small decorative type flowered in sprays.

Compact pale pink florets, pale golden centre. Upright habit, stiff stems, small foliage. Height 4 ft 6 in. Grown in pots in the open and flowered under glass in November.

334 **Yellow Tafetta.** 9c Y. U.S.A. Sport from Tafetta.
Small decorative type flowered in sprays. Compact clear yellow florets, deep yellow centre. Upright habit, stiff stems, small foliage. Height 4 ft 6 in. Grown in pots in the open and flowered under glass in November.

335 **Sylphide.** 7a P. WOOLMAN 1967. Preliminary Commendation.
Single type. Green and yellow disk. The ray florets reflex at the tips and are of a pale pink colour shading to white where they radiate from the disk. Stiff stems, small foliage. Height 4 ft. Grown in pots in the open and flowered under glass in November.

336 **Harriet Sherwood.** 7a LB. SHERWOOD 1965. Award of Merit.
Single type. Immaculate form. Green and gold disk, pale amber-bronze ray florets. Compact habit, stiff stems, good foliage. Height 4 ft 6 in. Grown in pots in the open and flowered under glass in November.

337 **Rose Cleone.** 7a P. BROWNSLAND 1956. Sport from Cleone.
Single type. Immaculate form. Green disk, soft rose pink ray florets. Compact habit, stiff stems, good foliage. Height 5 ft. Grown in pots in the open and flowered under glass in November.

338 **Flying Saucer.** 6a W. WALKER 1966. Anemone-centred type. Very large blooms of good form. A bold off-white cushion and refined pure white ray florets. Upright habit, good stiff stems.

Height 4 ft. Grown in pots in the open and flowered under glass in November.

339 Raymond Mounsey. 6a R. WOOLMAN 1950.

Anemone-centred type. Very large bold dome-shaped cushion with short chestnut-red ray florets. Upright habit, good stiff stems. Height 4 ft. Grown in pots in the open and flowered under glass in November.

340 Green Nightingale. 10 O. WOOLMAN 1965. Award of Merit.

Spidery type. Pale green quilled florets shading to a deeper green in the centre. Stiff wiry stems, good foliage. Very popular for floral arrangement. Height 4 ft. Grown in pots in the open and flowered under glass in November.

341 Jane Key. 9d PP. BEDENHAM 1970. Preliminary Commendation.

Single type flowered in sprays. Bright golden disk with green centre. The ray florets are of a soft shell pink. Compact upright habit, stiff wiry stems, small foliage. Height 4 ft. Grown in pots in the open and flowered under glass in November.

342–343, 344, 345, 346, 348 The **Shoesmith Salmon** family of Chrysanthemums is one of the most popular of the late-flowering types. They are at their best during the month of December. The parent from which other sports arose was introduced by the famous breeder, the late Harry Shoesmith. Each sport has all the good characteristics of the parent. They are vigorous in growth, upright habit, good foliage. Height 4 ft 6 in. Grown in pots in the open and flowered under glass in December.

342 Apricot Shoesmith Salmon. 4a LB.

Reflexing form. Warm light bronze florets.

343 Yellow Shoesmith Salmon. 4a P.

Reflexing form. Clear bright yellow florets.

344 Shoesmith Salmon. 4a P.

Reflexing form. Warm salmon pink florets.

345 Cerise Shoesmith Salmon. 4a Pu.

Reflexing form. Cerise pink florets.

346 Ruby Shoesmith Salmon. 4a P.

Reflexing form. Ruby pink florets.

347 Golden Rival's Rival. 5b Y. ROWE 1966. Preliminary Commendation.

Loosely incurving form. Broad smooth deep yellow florets with shining gold reverse. Hard texture, upright habit, good stems, dark green foliage. Height 4 ft 6 in. Grown in pots in the open and flowered under glass in December.

348 Bronze Shoesmith Salmon. 4a B.

Reflexing form. Warm copper bronze florets.

349 Rival's Rival. 5a LB. VINTEN 1956. Award of Merit.

Loosely incurving form. Broad smooth light bronze florets with amber-bronze reverse. Hard texture, upright habit, good stems, dark green foliage. Height 4 ft 6 in. Grown in pots in the open and flowered under glass in December.

INDEX TO COLOUR ILLUSTRATIONS

The numbers refer both to the colour illustrations and to their descriptions in the text

184